Michael J. S. Maher Jr.

Being Gay and Lesbian in a Catholic High School
Beyond the Uniform

Pre-publication
REVIEWS,
COMMENTARIES,
EVALUATIONS . . .

"Catholicism, since its great council in the 1960s, has moved from monolithic institution to diverse community. This is reflected in Catholic high schools that claim community, 'Christian Community,' as their defining characteristic. Yet, not all students who attend Catholic high schools feel part of these communities of faith, particularly gay and lesbian students. Michael Maher's groundbreaking book, *Being Gay and Lesbian in a Catholic High School*, speaks to this reality. Through real-world stories of real-world people, Maher explores the experiences of students who have yet to benefit from this communal vision of contemporary Catholic education. By breaking a code of silence that still surrounds too many Catholic high schools, this book challenges those who are responsible for Catholic education to live up to its ideals of tolerance and acceptance for all of its members. This book ultimately calls the Christian communities of Catholic high schools to a more complete faith."

Dr. Peter Gilmour
Associate Professor of Pastoral Studies,
Institute of Pastoral Studies,
Loyola University, Chicago

More pre-publication
REVIEWS, COMMENTARIES, EVALUATIONS . . .

"This is a book to be taken seriously by all who are concerned about high school youth, whether in Catholic schools or not. The silence on lesbian and gay issues must be broken. Too many lives are at risk.

If experience is a source for moral and ethical reflection, the stories of these students, with the pain and alienation they felt because of their sexual orientation, cannot be dismissed. Relying on Catholic Church teaching, Maher shows how a compassionate response to lesbian and gay adolescents is a moral imperative."

Sister Jeannine Gramick, PhD
Author, *Building Bridges:*
Gay and Lesbian Reality
and the Catholic Church

"Anyone who has had the opportunity to hear the experiences of gay and lesbian men and women know that they have generally received very little helpful guidance from priests and religious leaders. They have mostly been left to struggle with their sexual identity on their own. For many, high school was especially troublesome. The worst of their experiences led to great unhappiness, feelings of rejection, lack of self-esteem, depression, and, far too often, suicide.

At the very least, Michael Maher's book, *Being Gay and Lesbian in a Catholic High School*, offers the possibility that parents, teachers, counselors, and spiritual guides will be aware that there are gays and lesbians in every class of every school. His technique of sharing their lived experience through interviews is very effective. These are real people, and their suffering and struggle demand a compassionate and helpful response.

The task is made somewhat easier because there is more pastoral guidance from the Church leadership than there has been in the past. However, gays and lesbians and those who are trying to help them to a truly healthy personal development as homosexual individuals will not find much help from this leadership in resolving the inherent contradiction between being told that your sexual orientation is a gift, and yet a gift that you can never act on.

Maher has made an important contribution in setting forth so clearly what happens to young gays and lesbians in our Catholic high schools. Much more needs to be done to show how we can assist them in developing healthy, loving relationships within the reality of their sexuality."

Thomas J. Gumbleton, JCD
Auxiliary Bishop,
Archdiocese of Detroit

Harrington Park Press®
An Imprint of The Haworth Press
New York • London • Oxford

Being Gay and Lesbian in a Catholic High School
Beyond the Uniform

HAWORTH Gay & Lesbian Studies
John P. De Cecco, PhD
Editor in Chief

Behold the Man: The Hype and Selling of Male Beauty in Media and Culture by Edisol Wayne Dotson

Untold Millions: Secret Truths About Marketing to Gay and Lesbian Consumers by Grant Lukenbill

It's a Queer World: Deviant Adventures in Pop Culture by Mark Simpson

In Your Face: Stories from the Lives of Queer Youth by Mary L. Gray

Military Trade by Steven Zeeland

Longtime Companions: Autobiographies of Gay Male Fidelity by Alfred Lees and Ronald Nelson

From Toads to Queens: Transvestism in a Latin American Setting by Jacobo Schifter

The Construction of Attitudes Toward Lesbians and Gay Men edited by Lynn Pardie and Tracy Luchetta

Lesbian Epiphanies: Women Coming Out in Later Life by Karol L. Jensen

Smearing the Queer: Medical Bias in the Health Care of Gay Men by Michael Scarce

Macho Love: Sex Behind Bars in Central America by Jacobo Schifter

When It's Time to Leave Your Lover: A Guide for Gay Men by Neil Kaminsky

Strategic Sex: Why They Won't Keep It in the Bedroom edited by D. Travers Scott

One of the Boys: Masculinity, Homophobia, and Modern Manhood by David Plummer

Homosexual Rites of Passage: A Road to Visibility and Validation by Marie Mohler

Male Lust: Pleasure, Power, and Transformation edited by Kerwin Kay, Jill Nagle, and Baruch Gould

Tricks and Treats: Sex Workers Write About Their Clients edited by Matt Bernstein Sycamore

A Sea of Stories: The Shaping Power of Narrative in Gay and Lesbian Cultures—A Festschrift for John P. De Cecco edited by Sonya Jones

Out of the Twilight: Fathers of Gay Men Speak by Andrew R. Gottlieb

The Mentor: A Memoir of Friendship and Gay Identity by Jay Quinn

Male to Male: Sexual Feeling Across the Boundaries of Identity by Edward J. Tejirian

Straight Talk About Gays in the Workplace, Second Edition by Liz Winfeld and Susan Spielman

The Bear Book II: Further Readings in the History and Evolution of a Gay Male Subculture edited by Les Wright

Gay Men at Midlife: Age Before Beauty by Alan L. Ellis

Being Gay and Lesbian in a Catholic High School: Beyond the Uniform by Michael Maher

Finding a Lover for Life: A Gay Man's Guide to Finding a Lasting Relationship by David Price

The Man Who Was a Woman and Other Queer Tales from Hindu Lore by Devdutt Pattanaik

Being Gay and Lesbian in a Catholic High School
Beyond the Uniform

Michael J. S. Maher Jr.

Harrington Park Press®
An Imprint of The Haworth Press
New York • London • Oxford

Published by

Harrington Park Press, an imprint of The Haworth Press, Inc., 10 Alice Street, Binghamton, NY 13904-1580

Cover design by Marylouise E. Doyle.

Library of Congress Cataloging-in-Publication Data

Maher, Michael Jr.
   Being gay and lesbian in a Catholic high school : beyond the uniform / Michael Maher Jr.
      p. cm.
   Includes bibliographical references and index.
   ISBN 1-56023-182-3 (hard) — ISBN 1-56023-183-1 (soft)
   1. Homosexuality—Religious aspects—Catholic Church. 2. Catholic high school students. 3. Catholic gays. 4. Catholic Church—Doctrines. I. Title.
BX1795.H66 M34 2000
261.8'35766'08822—dc21

00-047216

1301-84-148

To David

ABOUT THE AUTHOR

Michael Maher, PhD, MPS, was born in Kansas City, Missouri, in 1967 and raised in the Kansas suburb of Roeland Park. There he attended St. Agnes Grade School and Bishop Miege High School. He attended the University of Kansas in Lawrence and earned a BS in elementary education in 1987 and an MA in religious education in 1991. He also attended St. Meinrad Seminary College in Indiana and completed the pre-theology program there in 1988. He earned his PhD in education at St. Louis University in 1997 and his Master of Pastoral Studies degree at Loyola University Chicago in 1999.

Dr. Maher currently serves as chaplain to the School of Education of Loyola University Chicago. He is also part-time instructor in the School of Education. Before coming to Loyola, he worked as a campus minister and as a parish director of religious education in Missouri. During that time, he founded two organizations, Passages: Greater Kansas City Gay and Lesbian Youth Services, and Gays and Lesbians Together at Northwest. He has served as the chaplain to the Gay, Lesbian, and Bisexual Association at Loyola.

CONTENTS

Acknowledgments

I wish to thank some very important people who helped me in preparing this manuscript. Most important, I wish to thank those people who consented to be interviewed. Although they are anonymous here, they shine through in their stories. I also wish to thank the officers of the gay and lesbian campus organization through which I conducted my university survey. Without their willingness to stand up to university authorities, I would never have been able to collect some very important data. In addition, there are some important people who provided feedback and direction throughout the study: Mike Grady, Paul Shore, Richard Peddicord, Mike Stanton, Tom Kopfensteiner, and Roy Cheatham, all of Saint Louis University; and Peter Gilmour, of Loyola University Chicago. I also wish to thank Mary Sperry of the United States Catholic Conference and Andy Roy, Jennifer Durant, Peg Marr, and Dawn Krisko of The Haworth Press for all their work editing the manuscript.

Chapter 1

Introduction

The specific mission of the school, then is a critical, systematic transmission of culture in the light of faith and by bringing forth of the power of Christian virtue by the integration of culture with faith and of faith with living.

Vatican Congregation
for Catholic Education
(1977, article 49)

I think in a way it just kind of built up a wall inside myself, like a place you don't go. The fact that it happened to be inside myself didn't seem to particularly matter.

Tom

Larry is excited about the upcoming homecoming dance. He is looking forward to spending time with some friends. It's a great year; he's class president and one of the most popular kids in his suburban, coed Catholic high school. He walks to the chapel for daily Mass.

Gina is a bit nervous about her presentation in religion class; she's chosen a controversial topic. Still, she knows that she has nothing to be too worried about. Her all-girls Catholic high school is a warm and welcoming place. She's apprehensive about leaving for college next year; she loves her school very much.

Mark breathes a sigh of relief as the bell rings for the end of the day. He's glad he's been able to avoid being beaten up at his small, rural Catholic high school today. He still has to ride the bus, so he's not completely out of the woods yet. "Faggot!" a student says to his face as he walks by in the hall. Mark thinks about killing himself.

Patrick sits up late one night in his high school seminary dorm. He's thinking quietly. The loneliness of his life as a new student is overwhelming to him. He wishes he had been at the school last year as a freshman. Everyone has already made friends, and the transfer students are being kept out of the cliques. Still, life is better here than at home.

Denise sits and has lunch with her clique. She likes the girls but doesn't feel that close to them. They're so different from her: Their parents don't have a whole lot of money, and they live here in the city near the all-girls Catholic school. She looks forward to meeting with some of her friends in the suburbs after school.

Although these students sound very different, they all share two things in common: all of them grew up to be gay or lesbian adults and all of them attended Catholic high schools. What is it like to be a gay or lesbian student in a Catholic high school? Given all the things that teachers and administrators in Catholic high schools have to worry about, why should *this* issue be important to them?

In the area of special needs of gay and lesbian students, researchers have shown some alarming trends. Gay and lesbian youth are at a higher risk than other youth for running away from home or being thrown out of their homes and living on the streets (Durby, 1994; Mallon, 1994). They are frequently victims of depression and low self-esteem (Savin-Williams, 1989, 1990; Schneider, 1989). They are at a high risk for suicide (Durby, 1994; Mallon, 1994; Friend, 1993; Massachusetts Governor's Commission on Gay and Lesbian Youth, 1993; Herdt and Boxer, 1993). One study conducted by the U.S. Department of Health and Human Services found that gay and lesbian youth are two to three times more likely to attempt suicide than other youth; up to 30 percent of teen suicides are committed by gay and lesbian youth (Gibson, 1989). They often avoid agencies that can help (Durby, 1994). Some gay and lesbian youth retreat into their studies and other activities, becoming overachievers (Mallon, 1994; Friend, 1993). Clearly, this population has special needs.

Why Catholic high schools? What is so important about this issue in *Catholic* schools? The American bishops' Committee on Marriage and Family sent a very important pastoral message to their communities in 1997 with *Always Our Children*. The committee told parents of gay and lesbian people that they must love their children. They told those working with youth in the Church that they must address the needs of gay and lesbian adolescents. Although the Catholic Church continues to condemn homosexual sexual activity, the magisterium of the Church has also called upon the Church to minister to gay and lesbian people and has made it clear that gay and lesbian people have rights in society and in the Church. Homosexual orientation *itself* is not sinful, and homosexual acts must be judged with prudence (Vatican Congregation for the Doctrine of the Faith, 1975, 1986, 1994; United States Catholic Conference, 1976b, 1991, 1997; Pontifical Council for the Family, 1996).

The focus of this book is a study I conducted in 1995 and 1996. I interviewed twenty-five (thirteen male and twelve female) gay and lesbian adults who had attended Catholic high schools in the 1980s and 1990s. On average, I spent about two hours listening to each person. I chose adults rather than current high school students for a few reasons. First, I didn't think I could find very many openly gay and lesbian students in Catholic high schools to interview. In fact, very few of the people I interviewed were open about *their* sexuality while in high school. Most gay and lesbian people do not "come out" while they are still in high school, so I think this group is representative of a sample of typical gay and lesbian students in Catholic schools. The focus of this study was to describe what it is like to be a gay or lesbian student in a Catholic high school.

In addition to this study, I also conducted two other studies that add a little more insight into this question. I had conducted a survey of 124 Confirmation candidates in the Diocese of Kansas City— St. Joseph in 1990. At that time, Confirmation was administered in high school. In this survey, I asked students to respond to sixteen statements regarding Church teachings on homosexuality. They were to indicate if they agreed with these statements. I decided to repeat this survey with incoming freshmen at a Catholic university in 1995. The survey went out through campus mail to students living in the dorms. Nearly 12 percent (103) of the students responded to the survey. I was able to compare students graduating from Catholic high schools with those graduating from non-Catholic high schools. (See Appendix B for tables from these survey studies.) In 1996, I interviewed a dozen counselors working in a variety of different types of Catholic high schools. I presented them with some of my findings and asked them to help me make sense of them. The findings from these two studies will be compared with the core study in the following chapters.

Catholic educational philosophy has changed throughout the past century since Pope Pius XI issued *Christian Education of Youth* in 1929. Catholic schools have been called upon to be more concerned with world issues. Students' personal experiences are to be part of the educational dialogue; this can, however, sometimes create tension with explicit moral teachings of the Church (Innes, 1992; Densley, 1991). Catholic education has a fourfold mission of community, service, message, and worship (United States Catholic Conference, 1972, 1979). Catholic schools must rely upon educational research, and greater research in Catholic schools is needed (United States Catholic Conference, 1976a, 1979, 1981; Vatican Congregation for Catholic Education, 1977, 1988; Vatican Congregation for the Clergy, 1971; Pope John Paul II, 1979). While the Church has the right to a role in the education of youth, youth also have the right to be educated and to play a role in their education (United States Catholic Conference, 1972, 1973a, 1979, 1980, 1981; Vatican Congregation for the Clergy, 1971; Vatican Congregation for Catholic Education, 1988; Second Vatican Council, 1965).

One theme that runs through Catholic educational philosophy in the statements of the magisterium is *integration*. Things are supposed to fit together as a whole in Catholic education. Academic studies are supposed to be integrated with students' lives and experiences. The faith should be integrated with academics and with students' lives. The students' home lives and families are to be integrated with the communities of the schools. Catholic schools are supposed to be communities into which individual students are integrated. I believe that this is one of the unique markings of Catholic education: the integration of student, studies, family, community, and faith.

The theme of integration makes the study of gay and lesbian youth in *Catholic* education uniquely important. However, in my interviews, I also found a theme of *dis-integration*—pieces not fitting together into a whole. This becomes very clear in the following story.

TOM

Tom* graduated from high school in 1988. It was a coeducational Catholic high school in the suburbs with about 1,000 students, run by the local diocese. It is safe to say that Tom was very shy, which seems to have shaped a great deal of his high school experiences. "I'd always kind of stick to myself. And I didn't know then—and I don't know now—how much of that has to do with the fact that I was gay. I'm sure some of it had to do with that."

Tom felt uncomfortable in the lunch room. He was too shy to approach people, but also didn't like eating alone. "I was just always self-conscious about, like, I couldn't eat by myself because if I did, that meant there was something really wrong with me. But on the other hand, I was really shy and couldn't approach people."

At that time in his life, Tom was aware on some level that he was gay. "I think I knew, but I just pushed it back. Like, 'I can keep myself busy with other things, like studying more.' I think I was always aware of it, but I was in denial. I wasn't acting out." He said he became aware of his sexual orientation at around age ten or eleven. "It was kind of by observation, like, 'Gee, that guy's cute.' It wasn't like, 'I have to have sex with this person!'" In second or third grade, Tom spent time playing with the girls in his school. He observed that someone must have told him to stop this behavior at some point, because he did. "I don't know if that has anything to do with being gay, but there are just certain things you don't do." He doesn't remember ever being attracted to girls; he had no desire to date girls in high school, and his parents never put any pressure on him to date. He didn't see dating boys as an option in high school. "I guess it kind of reinforced, 'Be by yourself. Be on your own.'"

None of his classmates seemed to view Tom as gay. He was never teased or called names by other students, with one exception. Once, a student called him a "faggot" in band class. "It didn't have an effect. It didn't change what I would say to people. It did make me think, 'Somebody could figure you out. Check yourself to see if you can find anything that's giving you away.' I guess it just kind of reminded me that someone could find out the truth."

---

*Throughout the book, all names have been changed to protect confidentiality.

In the interviews, we went a little deeper into how Tom felt about being gay when he was in high school. Tom's descriptions of his feelings are about the most clear articulations of dis-integration I found in my study. He gives a true image of a young person who is trying to put pieces from a variety of different puzzles together to make one complete picture.

"Being gay in high school was a burden in one sense, but, in another way, it was just a fact, and I had to get on with it. I just kind of looked at it like a characteristic, like being short or having brown hair. On the one hand, I was hiding it. But on the other hand, I knew it was not *the* most important thing at the time. That's what messes you up, because, rationally, you know, 'This isn't the most important thing about me, necessarily.' But then you get all this information and background that it's bad, so it just kind of blows it out of proportion. It should be an important part of you, but it shouldn't have to be inflated.

"I think in a way it just kind of built up a wall inside myself, like a place you don't go. The fact that it happened to be inside myself didn't seem to particularly matter. It's just a place that you don't go, like the teachers' lounge or something like that. I just accepted it and went on with my life. It didn't seem particularly bad that this place was inside *me*. I don't know that it was a sexual thing so much as just kind of, 'There's something I'm keeping a secret. I'm not going to talk about this.'

"I didn't want to torture myself by thinking about it all the time. I didn't think about it much. Of course, in everyday life, it comes up once in a while, like you see someone you find attractive or you see a straight couple walking together. It's like something you're grabbing at and pushing out of the way, but not really. When you're not, it pushes you back. It's kind of weird, you know."

One place Tom felt uncomfortable was in the boys' locker room. "I just wasn't sure if I was attracted to guys or not. I mean, I guess I was sure. It's almost like when someone takes something away from you and you feel like you need to hide again, or just kind of pull back." Nothing bad ever happened to Tom in the locker room, and no one ever teased him there, but he was uncomfortable undressing around other guys and being around other guys who were undressed. "Again, it's like one of those places where somebody could figure me out. I think that's almost the nature of being gay; what you do find attractive is at the same time threatening because you're too afraid to deal with it. It pulls you in two directions at once. You're attracted to someone and yet that kind of jolt just reminds you that you shouldn't be there or shouldn't feel that way. That's probably what messes a lot of people up."

Another place Tom felt uncomfortable was at Mass. "I guess in a way I felt like I was lying all the time, and church just kind of exposed that a little bit. You're supposed to be able to release everything when you're in church; God can see you for who you are." He also didn't like being forced to go to Mass rather than it being his choice. "I felt like I was celebrating something I didn't necessarily believe in. I felt like if I were myself I wouldn't be accepted in the Church. It wasn't like I hated God or something. It just felt fake. It didn't feel right or natural. I felt like, 'This isn't me.'" He also didn't like the social pressure to go along with Catholic rituals if they did not express what he himself was feeling.

I asked Tom how he knew at the time that the Church condemned homosexuality. "It was all kind of vague. It wasn't like I got a piece of paper in homeroom that said, 'We condemn homosexuals.' I never even really heard anything like that in Catholic school, but it was definitely a perception that I had and that I think other people had. You certainly didn't hear anyone advocating it as normal or healthy." He had some very strong feelings about the Church. "Change is difficult, but I just think the Church is getting to a real critical point where it's going to become an old relic that nobody pays attention to if it doesn't change."

In general, the topic was not discussed very much in his school. He remembered one "cool" priest who mentioned it once in neither a good nor bad way. One teacher mentioned in class that odds were that there were four or five gay people in the class. Tom thought to himself, "Yeah, you're right. There's at least one!"

"I wasn't naive enough to think I was the only gay person in the school." He suspected some people of being gay, but he didn't want to have anything to do with them. "They were just too weird for me." He had negative impressions of what a gay person was supposed to be like. "Weird, or strange, or kind of 'out there,' which didn't feel like me." Tom's peers never talked about gay people in any positive way.

Tom didn't feel that there was anyone with whom he could discuss these feelings. Students were required to visit the guidance counselor twice each year; Tom considered discussing it with a counselor, but he never did. The counselors never brought up homosexuality with him. "You don't necessarily feel safe. When you have something to hide, a neutral environment like the guidance office isn't necessarily going to bring it out of you. Other than that, there wasn't really anyone else to talk to or place to go. When I look back on it, it wasn't like torture. It was just like a roadblock. It never seemed like that much of an emergency. Sometimes it seems like until things get so bad, you don't really do anything; it's easier just to deal with it on your own until it gets so bad." Tom told me that although he wasn't sure if he would call himself depressed in high school, he was sad at times. When he went away to college, the pressure of coming out became very great. He dropped out of school and was hospitalized for depression.

When I asked him what would have made his high school experience better, he struggled to find an answer. Although Tom felt that things were a problem at his Catholic school, he believed things would not have been any different at a public high school. He wasn't sure if being more open about himself would have been better. "Being 'out' isn't one thing you do in one place. I don't think it would have made me happy to be out at school but not at home. I just don't think that would have made me happy in any real sense. It would have been nice to be able to talk to someone about it or to have been comfortable dating somebody. Society had to change before I felt I could be happy, and that's a real dangerous place to be."

In the following chapters, I present the stories of some of the other people I interviewed. I have divided these chapters into the different areas in which I discovered dis-integration. Each chapter also includes statements from the Catholic magisterium which define what Catholic education is supposed to accomplish in these areas. What will be clear throughout is that the goals of Catholic education are not being fulfilled for gay and lesbian students.

Chapter 2

Familial Dis-Integration

The first and primary educators of children are their parents.

Vatican Congregation
for Catholic Education
(1988, article 43)

*I guess that I don't feel loved anymore, at least not by my mom,
because she doesn't accept me for who I am.*

Gina

Church authorities have consistently emphasized the role of families in Catholic education. Parents are the primary educators of their children, and Catholic education is available to assist parents in this process. Parents are to be partners with the Catholic schools in which their children are enrolled. The home and the Catholic school are to be integrated. Not only is the education of their children a right of parents, but it is also a responsibility (United States Catholic Conference, 1972, 1976a, 1979, 1981, 1991; Vatican Congregation for Catholic Education, 1977, 1983; Second Vatican Council, 1965; Pope Pius XI, 1929, 1935; Pope Pius XII, 1951; Vatican Congregation for the Clergy, 1971; Pope John Paul II, 1979).

Parents' roles in the education of their children include sex education. Again, parents are to be partners with schools in providing sex education. Sex education begins first in the home (United States Catholic Conference, 1972, 1979, 1981, 1991; Vatican Congregation for Catholic Education, 1983). While parents can withdraw their children from sex education programs in schools, they are obligated to provide the same instruction to their children at home (United States Catholic Conference, 1991). Complete opposition to all sex education is in opposition to the Catholic Church's teachings. Children have a right to sex education (United States Catholic Conference, 1968, 1972, 1979, 1981, 1991; Vatican Congregation for Catholic Education, 1983; Second Vatican Council, 1965). The Church must provide sex education for parents as well as for children so that parents can better help in the educational process (United States Catholic Conference, 1981, 1991; Vatican Congregation for Catholic Education, 1983). In some cases, Catholic educators may need to intervene with parents in the sex education of children (Vatican Congregation for Catholic Education, 1983). Discussion of homosexuality must be part of children's sex education (United States Catholic Conference, 1979, 1981, 1991, 1997; Vatican Congregation for Catholic Education, 1983). The American bishops have instructed parents that they should tell their children about homosexuality as early as age nine (United States Catholic Conference, 1981).

In 1997, the American bishop's Committee on Marriage and Family presented *Always Our Children: Pastoral Message to Parents of Homosexual Children and Suggestions for Pastoral Ministers* (see Appendix A). This committee called upon parents to show love to their children. It encouraged parents to seek support services for their children and for themselves. This document was a landmark in the Church's pastoral support of families with gay and lesbian children.

How well are families integrated into the school life of gay and lesbian students at Catholic high schools? How involved are families in supporting gay and lesbian youth as they struggle to accept themselves? How are gay and lesbian youth in Catholic education integrated in their families? The three stories in this chapter show that gay and lesbian youth in Catholic education are typically *not* integrated with their families. They experience *familial dis-integration*. These stories, and all the stories in the following chapters, cover a wide range of topics and could have gone in almost any chapter in this book. I chose these three for this chapter because they touch on some important aspects of family life. Some of their problems with their families are related to their homosexuality. Some problems simply exist, but have an impact on the persons I interviewed. This is because they are stories from *whole* individuals, not individuals defined solely by their sexual identities.

PATRICK

Patrick attended a high school boarding seminary run by a men's religious order. Located in a suburb, the school was small and decreased in size while Patrick was there. When he began his sophomore year, the school had around 120 students. Only three years later, the school was down to eighty students. Patrick was a member of the last class to graduate before the school closed in 1984. He described the school as being very serious about preparing high school students for future lives as Catholic priests. Morning and evening prayer as well as daily Mass were required for the students. The school held many retreats, had a formation program, and provided spiritual directors. Drinking and smoking were serious offenses at the school, and students were not allowed to date. The focus was to prepare students for the seminary.

Patrick grew up in a small city in a nearby state. He wanted to attend the seminary starting his freshman year, but his parents did not allow him to do so; instead, he was able to attend beginning his sophomore year. Although a great deal of his motivation was a desire to become a priest, he also very much wanted to get away from his father. He explained that he didn't see himself as running away from his family problems, but just recognizing that he could have a better life at the school. Problems with his home life shaped a great deal of Patrick's experience.

Patrick's father frequently made homophobic comments. Patrick believed that this was because his father was actually bisexual but was never able to come to terms with that. He remembers a time when he was young, he came home, and his father called him into his bedroom. Patrick went to the door of the bedroom: the lights were off, but he could see his father masturbating. He did not enter the room.

"He would always talk about 'queers' and 'fags' with a lot of hate. And even as young as I was—a young teenager—I never let anything he said sway my opinions on the subject. I never let anything sink in as far as making his beliefs my own." When Patrick was in the sixth grade, Anita Bryant came to his city to help overturn the gay rights city ordinance. His father supported the effort. "And I'll never forget it, because I couldn't believe that he did that. I think I took it as an attack on myself." When Patrick was fifteen, his father made fun of him for looking inside a gym as they walked by. He ridiculed him, accusing him of trying to see the men working out in the gym. "I remember being so hurt by that. It was devastating. I kind of never forgave him for that." When Patrick was older, his father asked him if he was gay. Patrick lied, telling his father that he was not. Patrick's father was later diagnosed as a paranoid schizophrenic.

In his first year at the seminary, Patrick's life was not easy. He was one of a small number of students who transferred into the school after freshman year. Because cliques had already formed among the students, Patrick had difficulty making friends. He spoke to me in an almost haunted way about the extreme loneliness he felt as a high school sophomore. "I think the most threatening thing for me was probably the social rejection I felt sophomore year. That was the darkest thing. And I think it was probably the darkest thing I ever experienced in my life. I was so alone. I would just thirst for friendships there, the closeness. And I guess dealing with my own sexual awakenings and arousal, those desires were never quenched, so I was so alone. God, it was powerful! Very strong, very strong feelings of disappointment. I don't know if I was ever really depressed. I was just so lonely at times, sometimes profoundly." The best part of the day for Patrick was the sign of peace at Mass, when students would embrace each other. "I always looked forward to that, and I think it wasn't necessarily something sexual, but something that I needed. That human touch that wasn't in my life, I got there."

Patrick found support in a group of senior students. They recognized that he was having a difficult time fitting in, and they took him under their wing. He deeply treasured the words of encouragement some of them wrote in his yearbook. He read long passages from these to me. Many of these students he recognized as being gay. He also found support in his best friend, another sophomore year transfer student. His best friend was also gay and would point out gay students to Patrick, something he was too naive to do on his own. He also found comfort on retreats. He felt the "barriers were down" between students on retreats. He did not feel threatened in sharing (as some other people have reported) because they were allowed to write about very personal issues rather than share them in groups.

By his junior year, Patrick had earned more responsibility at the school and felt better about being there. He found his own clique. He described cliques at the school as small groups of five or six people who felt good about being together and also were very good at keeping others out. There were some traditional cliques at his school, such as "jocks" and "academic types." Most cliques tended to be based on personalities and familiarity, coming from the same towns. There were a few "gay cliques" but they tended to dissolve quickly. "I would say that there was a lot of gay activity, but I wouldn't say that anybody hung together solely for that reason." Some sexual relationships did exist between people in cliques.

Although Patrick was naive about sexual activity at the school his sophomore year, he became much more aware in his junior year. Students slept in large dormitories with only short partition walls dividing the rooms into cubicles. Older students were dorm prefects with a resident priest sleeping in a separate adjoining room. With little privacy, sexual encounters between students became readily known to other students. Phone conversations also could be heard between the partitions. Since students were also the dorm prefects, they tended to be more tolerant of sexual activity among the students than the faculty would have been, according to Patrick. He was a prefect beginning his junior year. At one time while Patrick was there, all the prefects were gay.

Patrick stated that sexual encounters were very common between students. He saw two reasons for this: a high number of gay students and the all-male environment. "I think, in my experience, at least, most priests whom I've met have been gay. I think gay teenagers would naturally be attracted to an all-guys environment." Out of the fifteen students in his graduating class, five were gay. In addition, many straight students had homosexual experiences while in school. "I don't think the lines were drawn. I just think people were interested in sex, and of course, being an all-boys school, there's going to be some messing around. And the faculty knew, but they didn't know how to deal with it. They couldn't lock us up all night. They couldn't forbid us to go on walks or anything. It wasn't like the old seminary days." He believed that part of the reason the seminary closed was the inability of the school's faculty and administration to deal with the prevalence of gay sexual activity among the students; they were too afraid to deal with the issue directly. Patrick went on to talk about what he knew about the lives of some of these students later. "I don't know anyone from my graduating class who's married now who did not have sex with other students in high school."

Although each senior was expected to take a freshman under his wing, sexual encounters between upperclassmen and lowerclassmen were not common, according to Patrick. He also believed that sex between faculty and students never happened. There was one diocesan priest who would go on trips with the students to the local pool for swimming parties. Patrick was disgusted with this priest because he would grope the students while pretending to horseplay in the pool.

Despite the prevalence of sex between students, and despite his own desires, Patrick never had sex with other seminarians while he was in school. He believed he was one of only three out of his graduating class of fifteen who did not. He said that this may have been due to his fears of getting caught or his own shyness. At times, it contributed to his loneliness, being one of only a few not in a sexual relationship at school. He worried that he was not attractive enough to have sex with other students. He did have some opportunities to have sex with students his senior year, but backed out of these. Patrick also was troubled by the conflict of desire for sex versus a strong sense of vocation to priesthood. He saw this as a distinction between himself and many of his classmates. "I don't think right or wrong was an issue. It was an issue for me, but I don't think, in my perspective, an issue for them." Patrick did not, however, judge his classmates for being sexually active.

Although Patrick did not have sex with other students while in seminary, he did have sexual experiences. Before entering the seminary, he had had some sexual experiences in junior high with other boys whom he had met through the Boy Scouts. He also had sex with men in his hometown when he went home during summer breaks. He met these men in a public park. Ironically, it was through his father that he had learned of this meeting place. "We'd go to the park and my dad would point and say, 'Queers!' So I knew where they hung out. That's the only place I knew at the time. I didn't know about any gay bars or anything. So I started going to the park. I can't say that they were pleasant experiences, but I did engage." This conflict between the vocation he was pursuing and engaging in sex with men became difficult for Patrick at times. "You could probably say I was a very confused boy at that time."

Despite all these experiences, Patrick still had difficulty describing himself as gay while in high school. "I didn't put labels on people, like 'gay,' 'gay,' 'gay.' But, looking back on it, I know that we were. It's difficult to explain. I wasn't in the habit of calling myself 'gay' or anyone else 'gay,' but I knew that we at least shared a common interest in men." He described his coming-out experience in college as "a very painful process."

Patrick was one of the few people whom I interviewed who saw his school as being progressive when dealing with homosexuality. Homosexuality was discussed in classes in a realistic and even positive way. Percentages and other information were provided in psychology classes. He felt that this was superior by far to the education he would have received at a public school. "I think it made me feel a lot more positive about myself and educated the rest of the students. We were so much ahead of the rest of the nation as far as our perceptions of homosexuality." The Church's condemnation of homosexual activity was discussed in theology, but put in context rather than being used as a condemnation of people. It was balanced with social science findings.

He felt that the tolerance of the school was in part due to a mostly gay faculty. Patrick received affirmation and positive perspectives on his sexual identity in spiritual direction. His director, a priest and faculty member, was also gay. Patrick only discovered this a few years after graduation. Although he appreciated the ability to talk about his sexuality in spiritual direction, he later resented the lack of direction he received from the priest and wished for the clear advice that the priest could have given him on gay life. "It was still something I was trying to figure out, I was struggling with, and all he could do was listen to me. If he would have guided me and helped me learn a little about myself, pointed me in different directions to reflect, maybe educated me in the real world out there. That may have been wrong, but I think it would have been better than just not saying anything. Maybe he was too afraid."

A few exceptions sullied the tolerant atmosphere. One priest was very homophobic, and Patrick said that the priest would not hesitate to expel a student for homosexual activity. Another exception was the coach. He had favorite students who were jocks, and he made homophobic comments about other students. He encouraged the jocks to go off campus to date girls. Patrick saw this as ironic because many of the jocks who the coach was sure were straight were also among the most sexually active of the students in the dorms.

One student having sex with another student did not justify expulsion. In reality, only two students were expelled for homosexual activity while Patrick was at the seminary. One student had a thirty-two-year-old male lover in a nearby city. Another had been very sexually active with a large number of students.

Patrick believed that the curriculum, the presence of many gay students, and the sexual experiences themselves helped many straight students to be less homophobic. There were some conflicts between gay and straight students; some students did leave the school because they felt there were too many gay people enrolled. Many of those who left also wanted to date girls.

Patrick was glad he had attended a seminary high school. He described it as "Healthier for me, without all the pressure to date girls and everything else." He was sad that the era of minor seminaries was over.

BECKY

Becky graduated from high school in 1989. She attended all four years at a coeducational, suburban Catholic high school run by the local diocese. There were about 500 students. She described her intense dislike of her school to me. Along with this, she was dealing with a number of family problems.

In her interview, Becky reiterated some of the same images of dis-integration that Tom recalled. "I think one major thing in my high school experience was the inconsistency. The inconsistency of my parents saying 'Oh yeah, we believe in all this stuff,' and yet my brother was molesting me, and they were, on some level, I think, aware of it and not doing anything. My dad was an alcoholic and was doing things that weren't really responsible, and yet we're going to church on Sunday." Becky's family was composed of stepchildren and adopted children. She described it as "a really insane environment." Her parents believed that one of her brothers was gay because he acted out in school by wearing eyeliner and strange clothes. "They already thought my brother was gay, so they definitely didn't want to hear it from me!"

Becky passed out in school once in the eighth grade. Her parents responded by sending her to a psychiatrist. She hated the man and described him as "a money hound, and all he wanted to do was put me on medications all the time." The situation with the psychiatrist also became a periodic problem between Becky and her parents. "Anytime I did anything my parents didn't like or didn't really understand, they'd say, 'Well, maybe you should go back and see your doctor.' They would pull me out of school for a month at a time."

Although Becky was aware that she had sexual attractions to women in high school, she didn't really identify herself as a lesbian at the time. "I didn't really have a name for it. Like, I thought, 'Okay, this is what I'm thinking about,' but it didn't really occur to me like, 'Oh, yes! I'm a lesbian, and I have an identity.' The whole time I was in high school I pretty much had a boyfriend. They were weirdo guys who were into watching pornos, and I would, like, watch these pornos with them and go, 'No, go back to the scene with the women.' And they were like, 'What's up with that?' I knew I was attracted to other women, but I didn't realize I had actual options, like dating other women. I thought the only option was getting married. I think the only time it ever occurred to me was the year after graduation, and I was at the skating rink with some friends. There was a group of women there who were obviously lesbians; they were holding hands. And everyone was like, 'Oh my God!' And I was like 'Oh my God!' but it was a different 'Oh my God!' If somebody would have shown me a picture and said, 'This is what a lesbian looks like,' I don't think I would have identified myself that way. I just figured I didn't like guys."

Becky was very critical of the pressure to date boys in her school. She saw this as part of a sexist structure in the school's culture. "Even I was preoccupied with boys. Part of it was that I really wanted to fit in. I wanted to go to the prom and stuff. My main goal was to get married and get out of my parents' house. It never occurred to me, 'I'll meet this great woman, and she'll have a great job, and we'll get married.' I mean, it was like, 'I need to find a guy who's gonna get, like, an MBA.' My parents really didn't want me to go to college. After high school, they just kept saying, 'Get married, get married, get married!' And I really didn't want to do that. I kind of thought I did, but then I started to realize that I could actually move out and not have to live with somebody. A lot of things like that they just didn't teach us. They didn't teach us it was possible to not go to school and live on your own. It was always, like, a man involved. It was like you moved out of your father's house and in with another man. And that was even in 1989!"

She really felt that the sex education in her high school was inadequate in preparing her for adult life. "They never really addressed real issues. They talked about, 'Well, if you're going to have sex, wear a condom.' They didn't say, 'Well, when the guy doesn't call you the next day, it's okay to feel like complete shit. You didn't do anything wrong.' They couldn't even deal with heterosexual sex in a realistic way. How were they going to deal with homosexual sex or even homosexual feelings without making you feel like a complete shit?" Becky had very strong feelings about a priest who taught at the school. "He wanted to be the cool guy, the cool teacher, and he just made fun of people and made them feel like shit all the time. And I was like, 'Oh, that's what Catholicism's all about.' There, too, I knew I never fit into that. I went through all the sacraments, and I went to Catholic school, and I wanted to believe it all, but it just didn't fit, and I think the homosexuality stuff was part of that. I read the Bible, and I knew what it said on some level, even though I never remember it being said in class. I knew that I didn't really fit into whatever it was that they wanted me to do. I knew that I didn't really want to get married. I knew that I really didn't want to have kids. I sure as hell didn't want to be a nun! So, it was really depressing. I mean, the Catholic Church, or at least the Catholic school I attended, really did make you feel like shit about having feelings that weren't heterosexual. Having feelings that were *homo*sexual, that could kill you!"

The silence on the topic of homosexuality in her school (aside from the frequent use of the term "faggot" as an insult) was especially troubling to Becky. "Homosexuality was never discussed in class. I kept waiting! I thought, 'Surely they have to talk about this somewhere.' And I thought we would talk about it in 'lifestyles' class. We talked about every kind of lifestyle except that one. I know the Church doesn't condone it, but just because you don't talk about something doesn't mean it doesn't exist! Even if they were to say, 'Well, it's okay you feel this way. Just don't act on it.' Well, no, that wouldn't have been fine. But at least it would have acknowledged that what I was feeling was real. They just didn't want to hear about it, and they didn't want to talk about it."

How Becky knew of the Church's condemnation of homosexual behavior was not clear. "I don't remember somebody saying, 'Oh, you're going to go to hell if you do that,' but it was definitely the impression that you got. I think if it's something that you don't ever, ever talk about, that's the impression you get."

Although Becky didn't recognize any other girls in her school as being lesbians at the time, looking back, she did realize that some probably were. "Basically, I just feel it robbed us of a huge experience we could have had. I mean, not necessarily sexually. Just the chance to talk about who we were." She did recognize some boys as gay. A number of them were friends of her brother. In most cases, it wasn't discussed between students. In one case, one student was very flamboyant. He was beaten and verbally harassed often by other students. Becky was truly afraid of experiencing similar treatment. Stereotypes were held by students, but mostly dealing with ideas of effeminate, nonathletic males. The female physical education teacher was rumored to be a lesbian "because she had short hair and muscular legs."

Despite this, Becky also said she was grateful that her sexuality was a little ambiguous to her while she was in high school. "If I had been more aware, I don't think I would have dated at all, and that would have been bad. And the pressure to date, all the dances and stuff, that was a huge thing in my school. If you didn't fit into that, that really left you nowhere." She would have had great trouble fitting in with her peers, and may have suffered abuse from students. "That guy, he got beat up a lot, and I knew that wasn't what I wanted. Plus, I really wanted to fit in." She advised that gay and lesbian high school students should not come out to their peers.

Fitting in was a challenge for Becky while she was in high school, but this seemed mostly to be her own perception. From her description in her interviews, it seems she had a great number of friends around her. "Even my best friend I wasn't close to. I always felt like there was something different, like I was missing something somewhere. I mean, I did all the regular stuff. I went to prom, I got decent grades. I could go the mall. I had sleepovers with friends. But I really wasn't all that happy, and I didn't get why. Now that I look back, I realize that I was doing a lot of things that I really didn't want to do, and I really didn't think I had any other options."

Becky also went through all these experiences alone; she never discussed them with anyone. "The dean of students and the guidance counselor were cool. Those were people I could have gone and talked to, but anytime you tell somebody something like that, they have to go and tell your parents. They would be really cool with you while they talked to you about it, but once they found out about it, you knew they would have to tell your parents; and your parents would really freak out. So, why would you tell anybody?" She said that she probably could have talked about it with her brother, but she "couldn't really put a name on it." She did describe retreats in the high school as "safe" but also not as a place where she could share her concerns about her sexuality. "Pretty much whatever you said on retreat stayed there, but also my boyfriend usually was there."

The experience of Catholic school left Becky very bitter with the Church. She said that she could not step into a Catholic church again. "To sit in a religion class and hear them say, 'Well, this is okay, and this is okay, and this is okay, and this is not.' At that point in my life, I couldn't distinguish between them saying 'That's not okay,' and 'You're not okay.' And it was really rough."

GINA

Gina was one of the youngest people I interviewed. She was a college freshman, having graduated from high school the year before, in 1995. She attended an all-girls school run by a women's order serving about 550 students. The school was located in an area that bordered between rural and suburban. She attended all four of her high school years at this school.

When I interviewed Gina, she was in a state of terrible turmoil about conflicts she was having with her mother. The two had been very close, "almost like best friends." A few months before the interviews, her mother opened a letter in Gina's backpack while Gina was home visiting. The letter to a friend revealed that Gina was a lesbian. Her mother confronted her with this information and became very angry. "I knew she didn't accept homosexuality at all from the way she was brought up. That was one of the reasons I didn't want to tell her yet—ever, whatever, but *not* yet."

The confrontation with her mother was very difficult. "She told me, 'I think it's wrong. I think it's unnatural. I don't think it's right. I don't accept it, and I never will!' And then she went into the whole thing about me kind of crashing her dreams of having grandchildren and the whole thing. I didn't really think about it from her point of view until she said it. So I tried to see it from her perspective until I realized that she wasn't listening to me and was never going to listen to me. I told her, 'You know, you have to think; this is sort of a new thing for me too,' and she was like, 'You said you've been thinking about this for as long as you can remember!' I realized that she was determined not to listen." Gina told her mother that parents should love their children unconditionally.

The issue of feeling loved was very strong for Gina. "I guess that I don't feel loved anymore . . . at least not by my mom, because she doesn't accept me for who I am." In a later interview, Gina reflected on this again. "I don't know that I don't feel loved anymore because I'd hate to think—maybe I'm in denial, but I'd hate to think that she doesn't love me anymore. But I don't feel the acceptance and unconditional support. I don't feel like she likes me." Her mother forbade one of her friends, Angie, from visiting the house. When Gina asked her why she was not allowed in the house, her mother responded, " 'Because I don't like lesbians.' And I was like, 'Okay. Where does that leave me?' "

Her mother took her to "a specialist." Gina went along with it, "humoring her," as she described it. Her mother found out that Gina had come out to a number of friends who were okay with her being a lesbian. Also, the "specialist" was okay with her being lesbian. Her mother became angry that everyone was okay with this. Things had recently quieted down between Gina and her mother as a result of talking to the "specialist." There were still some problems, however. "On the surface, everything's fine between us, but it's just not the same as it used to be. I don't know if it ever will be."

Gina's friendship with Angie was a turning point for her. Angie was a year older than Gina and attended another high school nearby. The two knew each other through sports and had been rivals in high school. They became friends in the summer after Gina's senior year. "Then she left for soccer camp, and I *really* missed her, and I didn't know why." Angie later wrote her a letter telling her she was a lesbian and asking Gina if she was also a lesbian. This was a very formative experience for Gina. "I called her the next day, and she talked about some of the experiences she had had. It was weird; it was like we were leading parallel lives. Like everything she said, I was like, 'Yeah, yeah, yeah!' When Angie asked me if I was a lesbian, I guess that was like the biggest turning point because I couldn't avoid it. It was like, 'Well, yeah. Yeah, I am.' So that was like a big deal, and from that point on, I felt like I really had to work at accepting it *myself*, you know. And I still am a little bit. It's all a process. I *had* to accept it for myself to be able to talk to other people about it. So I look back on how much time I've been thinking about this stuff, and it's, like, here's the first part of my life, here's Angie, and here I am now." Gina had a crush on Angie in the beginning, but then realized that they were meant to be "just friends." She valued this friendship greatly.

At college, Gina realized she needed to share her discovery with other people. She wrote a letter to another female freshman living in the next dorm room. "I just had this gut feeling I needed to tell someone. She read the letter while I sat there, and I just couldn't look at her. When she finished, I looked at her, and I could just tell by the way she looked at me that it would be okay. We talked a lot, and she almost thanked *me* for telling her. She gave me a hug, so I knew everything was going to be okay. When I think about it, I think of how lucky I am to have a friend like her. She knows everything about me and that's fine." Gina also decided to see a staff counselor at her college. This was also very helpful for her, but difficult. "I had to take the initiative in doing something to take care of myself, and I was uncomfortable with just the fact that I had to admit that I needed help. I didn't like that. I didn't really want to go to a counselor, but I knew that I needed to because at that point I hadn't told anybody. It wasn't like I was going insane or something, but I needed to talk to somebody."

Although most of what I've described of Gina's story have been events from her life shortly after high school, her life in high school was quite different. At the beginning of the first interview, Gina told me, "As far as in relationship to gays and lesbians and that sort of thing, I don't know how much anything really affected me at the time I was in high school. Because while, yeah, it was in the back of my mind, I didn't really realize that I was a lesbian until this past summer." She saw this also as related to her school environment. "Everyone in my high school comes from pretty much the same mold. It's so sheltered it's almost scary. Generally the same income, the same clothes, the same Catholic upbringing, the same Catholic grade schools, family, mom, dad, younger brothers and sisters. Not much diversity. There's *one* black girl there now. In general, anything that was different wasn't really talked about. It wasn't really a concern. As far as we knew, homosexuality didn't really matter, and there wasn't any need to talk about it. It just doesn't really exist for them. While it was in the back of my mind, nobody really confronted me with it, so it was almost like it didn't exist. Like I was trying to deny it, so I didn't really have an issue with it."

Gina was coming to an awareness of her sexuality in high school, but "slowly," as she described it. She did date boys while in high school. "I did it because I was supposed to do it. It was never really a big deal to me. I wouldn't get upset if a guy didn't call me up. While I dated quite a few guys, there was always something missing. Not that I didn't care about them, but, like, there wasn't a whole lot of substance to it. I guess ever since I can remember I've always looked at women. I mean, I have an idea of what a good-looking guy is, but I'd see a guy and look, but I'd see a girl and I'd *really* look. I didn't really accept that I was attracted to women at the time, when I was younger, but I knew it was something."

Small experiences of seeing lesbians did creep into Gina's high school life. She and a friend went to a coffeehouse in the city once. They did not know beforehand that most of the clientele were lesbians. "And my friend was uncomfortable, but I was like, 'Hmmm.'

And just little things, like if we went to a basketball game, a lot of sporting events, if I would see two women together, I would be like, 'Hmmm. What's going on there?' It was kind of fascinating."

Jokes about gay and lesbian people also would come up. In high school, she felt uncomfortable with these. "I was afraid to say too much, but I felt like a coward not saying anything. They probably came up as much as any diversity joke, but I was more hypersensitive to gay jokes. I didn't—I still don't let my mother tell Melissa Etheridge jokes. It's always been uncomfortable because either I never knew why, or I never wanted to admit why." While most impressions of gay and lesbian people that were common in her school were of gay men, stereotypes of masculine lesbians also existed. Gina said that she never really believed the stereotypes.

I asked Gina if she ever discussed her feelings with a counselor in her high school guidance office. "No, and I was really close to my guidance counselor. But the thought of talking to her never crossed my mind. I mean, *never*. I think that if I had talked to her, she would have helped. She would have tried to find a support group or whatever. You kind of had to go and find that stuff on your own. It wasn't like it was going to come to me. I think if somehow people had found out and rumors were going around school, she would have said, 'Hey, come talk to me.' But if it wasn't, like, that overblown, I would have had to go to her for help. It was just a very, very, very Catholic institution, and it just wasn't talked about."

She was also very close to her principal, one of the nuns from the order. She and her friends felt very comfortable with the nun and would visit her in her office after school. She knew, however, that the principal had had a negative reaction when another alumna came out. She stated that she wasn't sure how the nuns would react to her if she came out, but she was sure they wouldn't be encouraging.

Gina herself brought up the issue of homosexuality in her high school. In a senior religion class on social justice issues, she gave a presentation on homosexuality. "I remember I still didn't know that I was a lesbian, but at that time, I was really thinking about it. So it was kind of scary for me because I wanted to know more about it, but I was afraid to do it because I didn't want people to think, 'Well, is she?' As far as I know, nobody did. It was kind of scary, but I did it anyway." Resources on the topic didn't exist in the high school, so Gina had to use a university library to do her report. It was well-received by the teacher and the students. "That was what they said in class, but I don't know how true that would have held if I had said, 'Well, guess what!' "

"Anytime homosexuality would come up, usually it would be in the context of religion class. The teacher would usually give the textbook answer that the Church accepts the homosexual, but not homosexual acts. 'The homosexual is not a sinner, but when they act, they are.' It was never really talked down on. It was clear that the Church doesn't accept homosexuality and doesn't condone it. But it was also clear by their not talking about and avoiding it that you wouldn't really want to come out. The Church's teaching, quite honestly, I just thought was a crock. The way I looked at it was just like a backward Church thing, like a lot of things they say and do. I just find it hard to think, 'Okay, God loves everybody. . . .' That's what I was taught since kindergarten. I went to Catholic kindergarten, and I just cannot think, 'God loves everybody *except* for. . . .' And, to me, that's just kind of the message I got; 'He loves everybody, but you kind of need to work on this if you're different.' It's just an old institution, and it needs to get more liberal. I do have a friend who asked a priest what to do about having a lesbian friend. He told her, 'You have to love her no matter what.' It helps that there are people like that, but I don't think many of the religious are like that. I just don't get that feeling. The Church just needs to wake up!"

Despite this, Gina saw herself as very religious. "I never really thought that I was a very religious-type person, but I realize now that it was a big part of me. I don't know really the God stuff so much, but the community thing, just the support." She loved her high school retreats. She described them as "cry fests, and everybody's best friends on those. But junior and senior year it really carried over into regular school."

Gina also loved her high school very much. "My high school was all girls, college prep, private, Catholic, and, in general, it was very safe. My grade school was like that too, and I would say my whole upbringing was almost sheltered. I knew that everyone around me pretty much cared about what I was doing. Maybe I didn't agree with everybody, or was friends with everybody, or felt the support of everybody, but there were always plenty of people I could talk to. I really, really, really liked where I went to high school. There were groups of friends, but it wasn't cliquey, so I really felt at home. Any time I talk about it, I get real choked up. Because it was all girls, no one was afraid of what the boys might say or make fun of you if you raised your hand too much. One time, after a dance, I got drunk. It was the first time I ever did that, and I was scared. My friends took care of me, though. I remember I was never left alone."

As I stated at the beginning of Gina's story, her problems with her mother were a great concern for her. After one interview, she asked me a great number of questions. She wanted some advice on how to deal with her mother. She asked me a great deal about my relationship with my parents. She also wanted to know how to meet lesbians her own age. She was planning to start attending meetings of the college's gay and lesbian student group.

REFLECTIONS

I approach this particular area with some hesitancy. There are old notions still out there that some people are gay or lesbian *because* of family problems. Most people have rejected these ideas, and the social sciences tell us over and over again that there is no validity to them.

With Patrick and with Becky, their families had very serious problems which were not directly related to their homosexuality. This can also been seen in later chapters with Mark (Chapter 3) and with Nick and Dan (Chapter 6). While these problems are not related to homosexuality, the focus of this book, they are related to youth in Catholic education, also the focus of this book. As I've stated previously and again state, these are stories from *whole* persons, not just persons defined by their sexual identities. Consequently, some of the issues that they faced are more general to students in Catholic education and less specific to gay and lesbian youth.

None of the people I interviewed "came out" to their families while they were in high school with the exception of Mark (Chapter 3). In his case, it was against his will that his family found out about his homosexuality. Although some experienced support from their families as gay and lesbian adults, such as Emily and Bob (Chapter 5), the fear of being rejected by their families was very real.

Gay and lesbian youth are distinct from other minority groups of youth; they often lack family support in coping with their minority status and are often even oppressed by their own families (Friend, 1993). They must confront hostile environments in their high schools without family knowledge of their challenges and while fearing family rejection (Reed, 1992, 1993, 1994).

Fear of family rejection can have very serious consequences for gay and lesbian youth. It is a great source of anxiety for them (Gover, 1994). Savin-Williams (1989, 1990) has found that acceptance by parents has a positive effect on the self-esteem of gay and lesbian youth.

Normal adolescent distancing from families becomes abnormal for gay and lesbian youth. Parents sometimes blame themselves for their children's homosexuality. In some homes, the child's sexuality may be known but is denied a voice as family members refuse to discuss it. Gay and lesbian youth often fear being expelled from their homes, which can lead to a sense of needing to conceal their differences and an increased risk for suicide (Mallon, 1994). Coming out to parents can disrupt the youth's life (being thrown out of the house, etc.) and can disrupt the coming-out process itself. Gay and lesbian youth are more likely to come out to their mothers than to their fathers. Families from ethnic minorities or who are very religious often have greater difficulty dealing with a child's homosexuality (Herdt and Boxer, 1993). Homophobia in parents of gay and lesbian youth can be influenced by a number of factors, including how long the parents have known about their children's sexual orientation, authoritarian attitudes, attitudes about gender roles, number of gay and lesbian people the parents have known, and religiosity (Johnson, 1992).

DeVine (1985) has constructed a model of the stages a family goes through when reacting to a family member's homosexuality. These stages are influenced by how cohesive the family is, the family's spoken and unspoken rules and role expectations, and how the family views itself in social contexts. In stage one, *subliminal awareness,* the gay or lesbian family member feels isolated, and the family tends to avoid the topic. In stage two, *impact,* the family is clearly aware of the homosexuality of one of its members and begins to deal with fear and guilt. Bargaining and concessions come in stage three, *adjustment,* when the family realizes that they cannot change the homosexuality of the individual. Focus is on actions rather than the feelings of the individual, and the family tries to maintain its social image. Feelings of loss characterize stage four, *resolution*. In the final stage, *integration,* the family adjusts to the gay or lesbian individual and to his or her life. Another researcher has found that having a gay or lesbian family member tends to reduce homophobia in individuals (Watter, 1985).

In the stories of Mark and Nick presented later, the issue of violence in the home comes up. In Mark's case, it seems that it was at least partially related to his homosexuality. Researchers have found that gay and lesbian youth often experience family-related violence. Gay and lesbian youth are at a higher risk for abuse by family members and a higher risk for family disruption (The Child Welfare League of America, 1991; Vergara, 1985). One study of suicide attempts by gay, lesbian, and bisexual youth found that 44 percent of the youth attributed their attempt to family problems (Remafedi, Farrow, and Deisher, 1991). Hetrick and Martin (1987) found that 49 percent of their gay and lesbian youth clients who had experienced violence as a result of their sexual orientation were related to the perpetrators, and Hunter (1990) found that 61 percent of gay and lesbian youth who reported experiencing antigay violence were related to the perpetrators.

Clearly, gay and lesbian students in Catholic education face some very unique difficulties with their families. Although the Church expects families to be an integrated part of students education and sex education, in reality, families are usually silent at best and abusive at worst. Gay and lesbian students in Catholic education are not typically integrated with their families in very difficult times for them; they are dis-integrated from them.

Chapter 3

Social Dis-Integration

From the first moment that a student sets foot in a Catholic school, he or she ought to have the impression of entering a new environment, one illuminated by the light of faith, having its own unique characteristics.

Vatican Congregation
for Catholic Education
(1988, article 25)

"Safe?" That's a really weird word for a Catholic high school. I don't think there was anything safe. I mean, the only security I got was to hear that bell ring for us to leave.

Mark

The American bishops have identified community as one of the four major purposes of Catholic education (United States Catholic Conference [USCC], 1972, 1979). The importance of community in Catholic education is demonstrated by some of the statements from their *To Teach as Jesus Did: A Pastoral Message on Catholic Education.* "Education is one of the most important ways by which the Church fulfills its commitment to the dignity of the person and the building of community. Community is central to educational ministry both as a necessary condition and as an ardently desired goal" (USCC, 1972, article 13). "In this community one person's problem is everyone's problem and one person's victory is everyone's victory" (USCC, 1972, article 22). "Community is at the heart of Christian education not simply as a concept to be taught but as a reality to be lived" (USCC, 1972, article 23). The importance of community is re-stated often in other documents from the American bishops concerning Catholic education.

Although Pope John Paul II acknowledged that catechesis requires community in his 1979 statement, *On Catechesis in Our Time,* Vatican sources have not discussed the role of community in Catholic education to the same extent as the American bishops. Often, however, the "atmosphere" of a Catholic school is a subject taken up by Vatican sources. For instance, The Vatican Congregation for Catholic Education has stated that, "From the first moment that a student sets foot in a Catholic school, he or she ought to have the impression of entering a new environment, one illuminated by the light of faith, having its own unique characteristics" (1988, article 25).

Although community is seen by the magisterium as essential to Catholic education, how is this community experienced by students in Catholic high schools? In particular, how is community experienced by gay and lesbian students in Catholic high schools?

Again, dis-integration shows itself. In many key ways, gay and lesbian students are not integrated into the communities in their Catholic high schools. They are *socially dis-integrated.* When I was conducting my interviews, I asked each person to look through their high school yearbooks and create two lists: one they would call "safe" and one they would call "unsafe." Overwhelmingly, the issue of how well they fit into groups was the strongest theme that came out in this exercise. I would say that social dis-integration and identity dis-integration (Chapter 6) are the two areas in which dis-integration is clearest.

The following three stories I have selected come from very different students. On the surface, they seem to have had very different social experiences in high school. They did, however, share the same experience of "not fitting in" with their peers.

MARK

A number of the people I interviewed experienced different forms of harassment while they were in Catholic high schools, but no story was as dramatic as Mark's. Although I certainly cannot say that his story is typical, the fact that any person in a Catholic school suffered such treatment is very disturbing. Mark was in the high school graduating class of 1993, but he never graduated. He lived in a rural area and his high school was in a nearby town of about 5,000 people. He attended a public high school during his freshman year. Because he was being harassed there, he transferred for his sophomore year to the local coeducational, diocesan Catholic high school, which had about 170 students. Halfway through his junior year, Mark had to be hospitalized after having a nervous breakdown. He never finished high school, but he was attending a junior college when I interviewed him.

Mark began to discover his sexual identity in junior high. He remembers fantasizing about being a woman when he was a small child. He also remembers being emotionally attracted (rather than sexually attracted) to boys when he was a small child. Mark had also been molested as a young child. In junior high, he began to have crushes on some male actors and began to have sexual fantasies about men. He was promiscuous with girls in junior high, "just to make it obvious to peers that I was heterosexual."

By the time he was a freshman, Mark's sexual fantasies became very clear. Being in the boys' locker room proved to be a difficulty. Once, he was caught staring at some other guys while in the locker room, which triggered harassment at the school from some of his peers. Also that year, he found a boyfriend. When the two broke up, the boyfriend officially outed him to the school population. The harassment at the public school prompted Mark to ask his parents to send him to the only local alternative, the small Catholic high school. However, the harassment he received there proved to be much worse than what he experienced in the public school system.

The first couple of weeks were fine at the new school. Trouble began when the rumors from the public school worked their way into the Catholic school population. Also, unbeknownst to Mark at the time, he was exhibiting very stereotypical gay mannerisms. The result was escalating harassment from his peers. "It started out verbal, and then it progressed to other things—to physical harassment, to vandalism of a lot of my property. And it weaved its way into a lot of my life, to the point I was taking it home, and it got to the point that even home wasn't a safe place." Mark was physically assaulted by students an average of once every two days; he was verbally assaulted several times each day. Students frequently broke into his locker to pour perfumes into it. They also destroyed his assignments or wrote things like "faggot" and "sodomy" by his name.

Mark believed that part of the problem was the relative affluence of families who sent their children to the Catholic high school. They had more money than most people in the area, which Mark felt made their children spoiled and immature compared to students at the public high school.

When I interviewed him, Mark recognized that many of his behaviors were considered very stereotypically homosexual. During high school he did not realize this. One behavior was socializing with girls. "I always socialized with women, so this became a problem right off the bat because all the guys were homophobic. And any guy who did not socialize with the main group of 'men' was suspect—suspected of being homosexual." Mark was also friendly, quiet, and had a high-pitched voice. He had refined, effeminate mannerisms. He was prissy and stylish; he bleached his hair and used hair spray. He was arrogant. He walked with a swish. It's important to note that Mark described himself in this way. He also stated that he was not *trying* to act gay when he did these things. However, he did not change his behaviors when they became a problem; he said he had too much self-respect for that.

Mark was unfamiliar with most religious terms when he entered the Catholic school. He had always attended public school, and although his family was Catholic, they did not practice except to attend Mass at Christmas. The Catholic identity of the school contributed greatly to the type of harassment he received, according to Mark. "At that point, I didn't know what 'sodomy' meant, and they would say that to me. That's what I was called, 'sodomy.' That was my name. People knew that before they knew my actual name." Religion class also became a place where Mark was harassed. The topic of homosexuality came up about three times in religion class that Mark could recall, usually in the context of Genesis. "We would talk about Sodom, and, of course, no one could leave that alone; that was my name!" His instructor was a priest who did say that he had a friend in the clergy who was gay. Mark saw that as a positive thing, but it was overshadowed by the priest allowing other students to denigrate gays and lesbians. "He let them go on about how homosexuals should be burned. I sat next to a guy who looked right at me after he said this. And yet still saying, 'Stop abortion!' I mean, hypocrites!" Mark saw the Catholic influence of the school as being strongly behind the harassment. "I think almost 100 percent. This guy who sat by me in class mentioned that his pastor had preached against homosexuality in the Catholic Church there."

In one of the interview questions, I asked Mark what elements in his high school he would have called "safe." His answer was very disturbing. "'Safe?' That's a really weird word for a Catholic high school. I don't think there was anything safe. I mean, the only security I got was to hear that bell ring for us to leave. Even then, the bus ride to my car wasn't safe." He continued with this theme later in the interview. "Almost everything was unsafe to me, especially in high school. It was small, and so there really wasn't any place to go. It was very risky. Everyone was very unsafe to me; I had few friends. To me, it was like I was out in the wilderness. I was out in a jungle, and I had to fend for myself."

Mark was afraid to go into the cafeteria because food would be thrown at him. During lunch hour, he would roam the halls of the school because any of the areas where students would hang out were also places where he would be harassed. Teachers and school counselors were of little help. "Teachers weren't very sympathetic to what was going on. They were just like, 'Oh well, just find some place to go. There's kids in there. Just go in and sit down.'" Mark was particularly angry about the lack of involvement by teachers: "And what pissed me off the most was that every one of those teachers knew what was going on, and never once did they do one damned thing about it. They *knew* what was going on, what was being said to me. All they would do was just like a slap on the hand. They would go, 'Oh, don't do that. Try not to do it again.' Of course they don't give a fuck what these teachers say. They were going to go off and do it again and again and again. They didn't care. And that's what caused me to hate Christianity."

During his junior year, Mark discovered that a peer was about to tell Mark's mother that he was gay. After all the abuse, and with the threat of more abuse at home, Mark became suicidal. He wrote a note to a female friend in which he discussed being gay and being suicidal. The friend passed the note on to a school counselor. The counselor, in turn, passed it on to Mark's parents. "I couldn't take it anymore. I couldn't deal with the fact that my mother was going to find out. I was really thinking of just ending the pain and letting myself go."

Mark's family life was also a bleak picture. His mother had physically abused him from the time he was seven until he finally moved out at age eighteen. His father was also difficult: "My father was the type who would call gay men 'faggots' and 'queers' and 'sodomizers' and 'fudge-packers.' " When they found out he was gay, Mark's parents sent him first to a counselor, which Mark found was not helpful. "All it was, was, 'Don't worry about it. Just hang in there; hang in there.' I hung in there all I could. These little words of advice don't help anymore." Mark had been to psychiatrists before. By the age of sixteen, he had been to nine psychiatrists. His parents then had him hospitalized for depression. Mark actually looked forward to this. His mother hoped that they would "cure" him of his homosexuality. She was angry that Mark's counseling sessions were kept confidential.

When he was released from the hospital, he heard from his female friend at school that all the students knew what had happened. They planned to continue the abuse. He decided to drop out of school; his mother began her own harassment at home. She continually tacked newspaper articles about AIDS on Mark's bedroom door. Mark retreated into his bedroom, having meals there and becoming lost in movies he watched on the VCR. A married man in town had been arrested for molesting a mentally retarded child. Mark's mother told him that this would happen to him. "And she would be like, 'I'm just trying to protect you.' And I'd be like, 'No, you're not. You're trying to scare me into being heterosexual, something I cannot accomplish.' When I moved out, she was still saying, 'You're going to hell!' and 'You're going to get AIDS, because everybody else who is gay is going to get AIDS. That's how you're going to die!' At that point, I no longer trusted her."

Mark attempted suicide a number of times after he was released from the hospital. He also slept with a man who he knew was HIV positive. "I was trying to find someone who would care about me."

Mark stated that while he was growing up his family had not been very religious. "They are *now*, now that they know I'm a homosexual. They never go to Mass. They use Christianity as a weapon, though. They use it to their advantage when they want it. It's more or less a toy; it's a weapon. That's how I perceived it in my family and with the students." Mark himself never did identify as being a Christian. He said, however, that New Age spirituality had helped him in healing himself as an adult.

"Sometimes I look back and I'm just like, 'If I never went, I wouldn't be as strong as I am now.' But there's too many things I had to sacrifice, *too* many things. I mean, this is almost the first time in my life I've been able to talk about it without crying."

SUE

Like Mark, Sue lived in a rural area during high school. She commuted to school in a nearby town of 10,000 with a coeducational Catholic high school of 400 to 500 students. The school was the cooperative effort of a number of local parishes. She attended all four years there and graduated in 1987. Sue had trouble fitting in during high school, which resulted in some dangerous behaviors on her part.

"It was really a pretentious, narrow-minded school that didn't allow the students a lot of free thinking, which should be the basis of any high school. You're old enough in high school to form your own thoughts, and they really didn't like that." People in Sue's nearby hometown disliked her Catholic high school. "I was an outsider . . . I didn't get 'in' because I didn't go to grade school with a lot of the popular people. It was pretty cliquish and pretentious." She also felt that the administration didn't care about the students. They were interested only in the school and in punishing students who threatened anything in the school. "At the school, it seems, you were either judged on your athletic ability, your looks, or your money. Academics didn't even come into it that much."

Tensions with fitting in led to greater problems for Sue. "If I didn't like something, I either avoided the situation, slept through it, or took drugs. High school really got difficult for me my junior and senior year. I really wasn't bonding with anyone, felt out of place, didn't have any great friendships, and was sort of at odds with the administration and some of the teachers. At the time, it just seemed easier to sneak some of my mom's prescription pills to help me through the day."

Sue's awareness of her sexuality was undeveloped in high school. Much of it came as the absence of interest in boys rather than the presence of interest with girls. "It was pretty foggy. I realized that I didn't have a strong desire to date, but the word 'lesbian' never entered my vocabulary until I met Sally again, toward the end of college. It wasn't an option that was ever presented to me, so I kind of didn't even know it was out there. I'd say it was definitely there, but not conscious." (Sally had been Sue's friend in high school and later became her girlfriend in college.) Sue had an easier time making friends with guys than with girls in high school. She found them to be less competitive, more into sports, and not worried about makeup. "But the romance thing never happened, and that worried me, kind of. I just thought there was something wrong with me; I wasn't a sexual person or something." Around sophomore year, she did tell a friend she thought she might be gay. She couldn't remember what caused her to do this. The friend told her that it was only a phase and that all girls think that at some point. "And I just [said], 'Oh, okay,' and went on from there." She did experience some interest when she saw a friend naked in a community shower while on retreat her senior year. "It was probably a combination of guilt and excitement; something I shouldn't be thinking, but enjoyed thinking nonetheless."

There were some stereotypes of gay and lesbian people that the students believed. "When I thought of gay people in high school, it was totally about gay men. I probably laughed at gay jokes, but never told any. I don't think I felt any hostility, like that gays were unnatural or something like that. I really didn't meet a gay person until college, and I'm sure in high school I thought of the effeminate man or the bull-dyke woman. Plus, girls in high school who didn't date anyone—if guys couldn't get a date with them, they made jokes about them being dykes. That probably helped to form my first impressions of sort of antisocial or negative women who had facial hair."

Dating pressure was strong. Sue felt bad about herself for not having a date for the prom. "A lot of people thought less of you if you didn't have a date." She also felt uncomfortable with homecoming queens and cheerleaders. "Only the popular girls were voted in and also it was pretty stereotypical. They were just choosing women for their physical appearance. It was all pretty shallow."

Her girlfriend at the time of the interview was Sally; neither Sue nor Sally had been aware of their sexuality in high school. Sue also had two female friends in high school who came out later in college. None of them were out in high school, but rumors circulated about her two friends. When I asked her if she ever compared herself in high school to these two friends who people gossiped about, she told me, "I really didn't feel like I related to anyone in high school."

Sue greatly disliked what she interpreted as the school forcing beliefs onto students. She described one priest who taught in the school as a robot. "Whatever the Church or pope said was what he thought and what he said. He couldn't form any independent thoughts." She also disliked another priest who taught in her school. "He just lived by the dogma, and didn't think for himself. He taught a slanted course in world religions. I remember questioning him on some things, and he just kind of laid down the law and—just a 'don't argue with me' kind of thing." She disliked Masses at the school. "Basically it was forced attendance, and I found it to be ritualistic and unfulfilling spiritually." She also didn't like the pro-life club. "I just didn't like that they didn't try to explain both sides of the situation to help you make a choice for yourself."

Teachers taught that homosexuality was a sin in religion classes. "The Church's current policy, I feel, produces a lot of hate and intolerance, which is kind of ironic because being lesbian or gay, a lot of it's about love. And the Church doesn't understand that. It's too bad."

Sue did see some positive aspects of her high school. She stated that the school did encourage girls to go on to college despite the local culture of the town that encouraged girls to get married after high school. Some extracurricular activities encouraged boys and girls to socialize together in sports and other activities. A liberal political organization at the school was open for students. Boys in the school could take home economics classes without any stigma. Sue also found outlets for herself in the school's theater department.

LARRY

Larry graduated in 1981 from a coeducational, suburban Catholic high school of about 900 students. It was run by the local diocese. His story is somewhat different from those of Mark and Sue. Larry enjoyed great popularity in his high school and was class president. Despite this, some common themes emerge among these stories.

Larry played the role of a joker in high school. He was very popular with many people, especially many girls, because of his sense of humor. Larry still felt tension fitting in, however: "Even though I was in the mainstream, I was sort of suspicious of it." Many of the close friends he chose were also special people who disregarded the social rules of peer pressure. He described them as "alternative" and "artistic." Larry described one of his friends at the time: "She was extremely beautiful and really bright, and all the popular girls wanted to hang out with her. But she wanted to hang out with the punk rockers. And she did funky things like corn-row her hair." He also felt very comfortable with teachers who didn't "fit the mold." Teachers who were liberal and artistic were his favorites for the most part, such as the one he describes here: "She was one of the few funky, alternative people who taught at the school. Most of them were sort of ex-student council presidents who couldn't grow up." Larry discovered that many of these students and teachers lived in the city and had gay friends in their neighborhoods.

He noted that female friends were very important to him in high school. "I got teased about that a little in grade school, but when I look back, it was those friendships with straight women that were most important to me at the time. It is still true to some extent in my life today. I think that really helped me. That may be why it's harder for gay male students in all-male schools; they don't have as much opportunity for friendships with straight women."

Despite this closeness to girls, dating was uncomfortable for Larry. He described dances at his school as "Exclusionary. I was actually one of the homecoming kings at my school. But the whole atmosphere is sort of mandatory heterosexuality, and if you're not heterosexual, then you're posing [as one]. While I was extremely popular in high school, I could have taken probably just about any girl I wanted, but by senior year I was fairly aware that I didn't have an interest in it the way my male peers did. I would always get around it by taking a girl who was just a good friend. One time, I went to a turnabout dance with this girl who was interested in me. At the end of the night, I know she wanted a kiss. I didn't want to, so I just gave her a little hug.

I could tell she was really annoyed with me. I think it was my senior year that a guy took his male date to [the] prom. I remember having this admiration for him."

One male friend, Bill, stood out as being important to Larry. "I think Bill always knew that I didn't like girls. He never pushed it on me. Other guys were pressuring me to date, and he'd be like, 'Oh, do what you want.' I came out to him shortly after high school, and he was not at all surprised. I sort of had real issues because I had this bad sort of crush on him." The crush confronted him one night: "I remember one night us getting drunk and fighting over a sleeping bag. We were both in our underwear. And we were wrestling over it, and I can remember feeling myself getting hard. I said, 'Here, you can just have it.' I grabbed a pillow and rolled over onto the floor so he wouldn't see it."

Fear of similar incidents shaped some of Larry's socializing. "I think probably in a number of ways that fear of arousal caused me to pull back from guys in a number of contexts. I can remember not wanting to get drunk, not wanting to get stoned, because I was afraid that if I did, that some way [it] would come out, that I would say something or do something. I was so guarded all the time to make sure that wouldn't happen."

Larry did recognize some of his peers as gay when he was in high school. "It reminds me of this joke that a comedian told: 'They had a head start program for gays in my high school. It was called Drama Club.' The kids who did the plays at my high school were very much picked on. It was sort of like real queer to do it. The guys there, they were all kind of nellie [effeminate]. They were all very, very nice, and I always felt comfortable around them, but I never took part in the plays because I never wanted to be associated with them. I would go to all the plays, and I went to their cast parties and stuff. There were always rumors about the guys there, but I was real liberal, so I'd be like, 'Well, it's okay for *them* to be that way.'"

One student was openly gay. Larry did not have fond memories of this person. "He was obese and had long, goofy hair. He was the first person I ever knew who admitted he was gay, and people wanted to beat him up and would make fun of him. He actually told people that he had gotten out of a speeding ticket by sucking the cop's dick. He was walking around school telling people this! He was *extremely* effeminate. That was my first impression of what it was like to be gay, and I was mortified. I just thought of gay men as extremely effeminate, sort of Charles Nelson Reilly-type men."

One group of males did make Larry feel threatened: the football team. Some of them called him a faggot; his freshman year, they tried to hurt him when his P. E. class played football. He associated sports with fear for two reasons. The first was his fear of being threatened by "jocks." The second was his fear of arousal in situations involving physical contact or showers with other boys. "I'm sure they thought I was a fag. I think most other people just thought I was kind of a sensitive, nice guy. I really worked hard at controlling things—controlling how I acted, how I spoke, that kind of thing. I had a real fear, too. Just below the surface, I felt frightened by my own sexuality and about the fantasies I had about the other boys." Larry saw this as having a long-range effect on his attitudes toward sports. "I avoided sports and athletics and had stayed away from sports and just thought of myself as unathletic because I wasn't really good at those things, and those guys discouraged me from participating. They were really cruel to me in some of those contexts. I was twenty-five years old before I did anything athletic again. It was a major battle just getting myself to go to a gym again. Even now when I work out and I go into the locker room and the weight room and there are a bunch of jocks in there, it still makes me a little nervous."

Larry had some interesting thoughts on his harassment by his peers. "They kind of figured that I was gay, and they called me 'fag' or 'sissy' or whatever, but I don't think they ever really thought that I would have sex with a man. I think a lot of times in Catholic high schools, when they call you 'fag' or 'sissy,' they really mean that you're effeminate, and, hence, different. To think that people would actually engage in gay sex was probably a little much for them. I think they really mean something else. They all knew something about me was different, and they made me deal with those feelings of being different; they sort of rubbed my face in it. I avoided them. I said mean things about them. I became sort of catty."

Larry had reframed much of his thinking about being threatened by this group and about dating pressure. "The couples at [the] prom, and the exclusionary way that made me feel, at the time, I felt sort of 'less than.' I just felt really different. I still feel that way if I'm at a wedding or at a restaurant in the suburbs. I become acutely aware that I'm gay, and I'm not like these people. I sort of reframed that, and now I'm thankful that I'm not like these people. I don't have to live their stifling, ghastly lives. I'm not stuck in their pre-fabbed lives. They don't have much of a chance to invent themselves; their lives are pretty scripted. Once I got over the pain of not being some of those guys—those guys who made fun of me, I began to sort of revel in the fact that I wasn't one of them. It's like, Jesus! I wouldn't want to be one of these guys! They're the kind of people who voted for Ross Perot. They never did anything past high school. One of them works for his father-in-law's insurance company. These are people who are not cultured, not intellectual, not witty. There's nothing about them I would want to be. I became aware of my own difference, and then I liked my identity. I'm certainly past that at this point in my life. I don't need to hate them. I don't need to put them down in order to like myself, but I think at the time I did. It sort of gave me a false sense of superiority or a smugness, but probably one I needed at that time."

I asked Larry to further elaborate on his comment, "getting over the pain of not being some of these guys." "I think there was always a part of me that wanted to be the butch, athletic, all-American-boy type that I never was. I mean, isn't that why gay men are in the gym six nights a week working on their lats? There's this part of us that wants to recreate something that we never were. I was sad through much of my childhood that I wasn't one of those jock boys like the other boys and like what my dad wanted me to be."

Larry's sexual awareness was elusive for him in high school. "I knew something was different about me when I was a small child and used to work out dance routines to 'Gypsies, Tramps, and Thieves' with my sister. My awareness of my homosexuality was just sort of below the surface. So was this sadness—the sadness of feeling different. I had a sense that I couldn't do those sorts of things; I hardly ever went on any dates. If I did date, it was very uncomfortable. I knew I didn't want to be sexual with a girl. Yeah, there was a certain sense of sadness about my difference. I think at the time I probably dealt with it by probably some denial. I tried to suppress it. There was probably some sublimation. That's probably why I became a good college student, and a workaholic in some ways. And I cultivated a lot of really good friendships. I was older—I was twenty before I ever became sexual with somebody. When I was fourteen to sixteen, I viewed it as a phase. After that, I just pushed it into activities and homework and friendships until I was a junior in college. I was having so much fun in high school. When I was having fun, and studying, and doing all the things you do in high school, participating in activities, I think I felt pretty much like everybody else. Sometimes things would happen that would bring about more self-awareness. That was strange, though. That's the thing about denying your sexual orientation; I could masturbate thinking about some guy, and still not think about myself as gay. But I also remember one night going to a football game and one guy called me a faggot, and I thought about it for weeks. I sort of obsessed about it."

Larry had been very religious in high school, but he became an agnostic in college. This did not seem to be strongly related to his homosexuality, however. "I went to Mass every day of Lent for all four years. I went to Mass for every first Friday from first grade through senior year. I was really religious that way." It was in the later part of college that Larry quit the Church. "I quit the Church over both theological and political issues, but not homosexuality. That pissed me off, and was maybe the straw that broke the camel's back, but I was much angrier about abortion and the Church's stance on women. Also, it just didn't make sense to me theologically." Larry had no awareness of the Church's statements on homosexuality when he was in high school. "I *never* thought about it. I never dreamed that this was an issue in the Church. I don't recall it ever being mentioned in any classes. I never felt like I got a message that was antigay. I really didn't. Certainly some of the issues around gender and masculinity, but never *specifically* antigay."

Larry did have some negative feelings toward most of the faculty and administration. "I have this impression that the administration at my high school was just very judgmental. I have a feeling that they didn't like anybody or anything that was different. I would not have called them homophobic as a senior in high school, but I knew they were conservative. I had a sense that there was a rigidity about them."

Larry told a story about one teacher that was particularly disturbing. She was a nun, and Larry also believed at the time that she was a lesbian. "I remember one time in front of a class she said to me,

'Larry, did you leave a sweater here?' And I said, 'No, I didn't.' And she said, 'Well, I found this one, and I thought it might be yours.' And she held up what was obviously a girl's sweater. I think it was a really obvious attempt to try to shame somebody, and I think it was a projection about her own sexual contention and her discomfort with that. She was a pretty fucked-up woman. She was really bitchy to me, but I think I realized fairly early that she was probably a frustrated lesbian, and I had more sympathy for her. I think she was pretty fucked up. I mean, I get annoyed sometimes when I think about some of those teachers, but I think they're pretty limited in some ways, so I sort of let it go."

One teacher stood out because of the concern he showed for Larry. "He was one of the religion teachers. I felt safe around him. He was really kind to me after my dad died when I was a freshman. And he was sweet and supportive and did a lot of extra things to connect with me. He was just sort of a typical guy. I mean, there was nothing extremely different about him. I suppose he was more liberal than most of the other teachers, maybe a little brighter. But I think he was just compassionate."

Although Larry did not view his school as overtly homophobic, he did believe that the Catholic culture contributed to a rigidity and gender conformity in the school. "A lot of conventions at my school I now see as deeply related to gender issues and deeply related to Catholicism. Having gone to a Catholic school where there's a great rigidity in terms of the rules and structure and authority, I think that may be why some people feel so much anger who come from Catholic backgrounds. So much of it just feels arbitrary. It influenced me into much more democratic thinking as an adult, and liberal thinking. I'm a socialist now. I'm a feminist because I think of those power differentials and the impact they have on peoples' lives."

As part of the interviews, I asked Larry what changes would have made his high school experience better. He suggested that the students and faculty needed some training on a range of diversity issues. He also felt he needed more role models and that the curriculum should be changed. He made suggestions such as adding noncompetitive athletics options for boys' physical education. He would have liked to have experienced less dating pressure. "If I could have somehow known my future was going to turn out okay—if I could have met adult gay men who had decent, constructive, productive lives. I had a Christian marriage class that absolutely helped me in no way to think about my adult life. Catholic schools seem to have this real naive sense that their students are all the same. I see them as narrow and closed-minded. I think, in some ways, it's probably not a matter of education for the people who run Catholic schools. I suspect that most of the things I've mentioned they probably know. They need to think about the implications of those things morally and ethically."

REFLECTIONS

Some key themes from these three stories and from the interviews in general can be addressed here. Probably the most important theme is that of not being close to one's friends. This seems to stem from two conditions: one is simply not having many friends, as in the cases of Mark and Sue; the other is having friends but still feeling detached from them, as in the case of Larry.

A distinction should be drawn between Mark and Sue. For Mark, his lack of friends clearly was related to being gay. Fellow students ostracized him for this reason. Was this the reason Sue also lacked friends? It does not seem to be the case. For several other individuals I interviewed, however, their feelings of not fitting in were very threatening. Although all high school students feel isolated from some of their peers, this does not diminish the importance of this theme in terms of gay and lesbian students. It is possible that gay and lesbian students feel social isolation in a different way than their straight peers. It must again be noted that *whole* persons are being discussed in this study, not just persons in terms of their sexual identities. Consequently, some themes that have emerged from these interviews will be common to many Catholic high school students, not just gay and lesbian students.

Larry's experience also deserves closer examination. Did he feel detached from many of his fellow students who seemed to be his friends *because* he was gay? In some cases, this seems to be clear. Larry felt uncomfortable about his lack of interest in dating girls and the social stigma that implied. Another person I interviewed, Emily (Chapter 5), made this point even more clearly. Like Larry, she was very popular in school; however, "I didn't like the fact that everyone loved me for who they thought I was, but nobody *really* knew who I was."

This feeling of isolation has been the subject of some research. The belief that, "If others really knew me, they wouldn't like me" contributes to low self-esteem in many gay and lesbian youth (Friend, 1993). High school exerts a strong pressure on gay and lesbian youth to conform (Herdt and Boxer, 1993). Faced with a decision between being invisible or being outcasts, gay and lesbian youth have a greater sense of being alone than other teenagers (Vergara, 1985). Their efforts to hide their sexuality may take a great deal of time and energy and affect their entire lives. They tend to give their sexuality "global significance" because of the attention it requires in their lives (Durby, 1994).

Larry's situation also calls attention to the fact that almost all of the people I interviewed did experience integration with peer groups in some ways. Many examples are presented noting how these people found friends in high school. Sometimes, this was done when certain boundaries could be broken down. Allen (Chapter 5) was not athletic, but he became a part of the baseball team at his school by being the photographer who traveled with them for their games.

Several of the people I interviewed felt that their relationships with peers improved in the later years of high school. It seemed that the social norms of high school freshman are much harder on gay and lesbian students.

My survey results provide some important insight into the attitudes of students in Catholic education. Although all the items on these surveys are designed to show students' attitudes toward gay and lesbian people and the Church's responsibility to them, one item is especially helpful here, "Gay and lesbian people deserve friendship." In the 1990 study of high school Confirmation candidates in the Kansas City–St. Joseph Diocese, only 52.9 percent of males and 88.9 percent of females agreed with the statement. A full 100 percent of females expressed agreement with this same statement in the 1995 Catholic university freshmen study, but only 77.4 percent of males agreed with it. At least with male students, it is clear that peer attitudes inhibit development of meaningful friendships with fellow students who are gay and lesbian in Catholic high schools.

There have been a few other studies that have sought to discern attitudes of Catholic teenagers regarding homosexuality. A 1981 study found that 77 percent of American Catholic youth agreed that sex between two adults of the same sex was wrong. The study also found that attitudes of Catholic youth were not significantly different from those of Protestant youth (Fee et al., 1981). Similar results emerged from a 1986 study of seniors at Catholic high schools in the Archdiocese of Washington, DC. Only 30 percent of the respondents agreed that homosexuality was an acceptable life style (McAuley and Mattieson, 1986). Attitudes appear to have shifted over time, however. A longitudinal study of seniors at one Catholic high school found that their support for a city ordinance protecting gay and lesbian people from discrimination grew from 44 percent in 1977 to 52 percent in 1989. Although this increase was only from 50 percent to 53 percent for female students, the male students increased from 35 percent to 50 percent (McNamara, 1992).

This last statistic deserves comparison with my own surveys. As noted earlier, the 1995 survey of freshmen at a Catholic university indicates that students graduating from Catholic high schools showed more positive attitudes toward gay and lesbian people and toward homosexuality than those graduating from non-Catholic high schools. The 1990 study of Confirmation candidates indicates the greater the number of years males spend in Catholic education, the more likely they are to agree with Church teaching on homosexuality, including positive statements by the Church. It seems that although males' attitudes toward gay and lesbian people are generally more negative than females' attitudes, they are also more changeable through life experiences and education.

A number of broader studies have been conducted in the area of attitudes toward homosexuality and gay and lesbian people. George Weinberg (1972) is credited with coining the term, "homophobia." Although this term is used often when describing negative attitudes toward homosexuality, it may be a misnomer in many cases. Studies have shown that while fear ("phobia") is a factor in some peoples' negative attitudes toward homosexuality, not all negative attitudes can be attributed to fear (Herek, 1985a, 1985b; Plasek and Allard, 1985). The term "heterosexism" has also been used to describe negative attitudes toward homosexuality (Friend, 1993). One finding that

seems to be universal is that males tend to have more negative attitudes toward homosexuality and gay and lesbian people than females
(Herek, 1985b; Aguero, Bloch, and Byrne, 1985; Reinhardt, 1995;
Kite, 1985; D'Augelli, 1989; D'Augelli and Rose, 1990; Newman,
1985; Hansen, 1982; Watter, 1985; Wells, 1989). The AIDS epidemic
also has increased negative attitudes toward homosexuality in our society (Ellis, 1989; Russell and Ellis, 1993; Walters, 1990; McDevitt,
1987; McClerren, 1992). A number of correlations between attitudes
about homosexuality and other factors have been studied by researchers. Interestingly, Herek (1985b) found that people who have negative attitudes toward gay and lesbian people have much more strongly
negative attitudes toward gay and lesbian people whom they perceive
as being most like themselves.

Returning to the people I interviewed, Larry mentioned his realization that a gay clique existed in his high school in the drama club. Sue
also discovered later, in college, that several of her friends in high
school were lesbians. The existence of gay cliques in high schools
was mentioned by some of the people I interviewed. These cliques
did not seem to form around the issue of being gay or lesbian, but
some seemed to simply have more gay and lesbian people in them,
such as the drama clubs and the girls' softball teams. There were
mixed reactions to these groups. Some of the people I interviewed in-
tentionally avoided groups that were thought to have a great number
of gay and lesbian students in them; they worried about "guilt by association." Others, such as Patrick (Chapter 2) found comfort in being a part of such groups.

While gay and lesbian youth go through the stages of "coming
out," they eventually reach a point when they feel they must meet
other gay and lesbian people. This helps to make being gay or lesbian
a more normal experience and provides the young person with information they might not find through other resources (Cass, 1979). The
need of some gay and lesbian youth to meet other gays and lesbians
can be very difficult; most routes to socialization are closed to mi-
nors. As a result, some gay and lesbian youth find themselves seeking
socialization in adult situations which can be erotically focused, such
as with Patrick (Chapter 2) (Durby, 1994). This type of transition is
difficult for many young people. In a study of adolescent lesbians,
Schneider (1989) found that many young lesbians had difficulty

transitioning from hanging out at the mall with friends to hanging out in a lesbian bar. Many of them did not like bars. Contact with other lesbians, however, removed some of their sense of isolation and increased self-esteem. Many cities have gay and lesbian youth groups, and these have been shown to be important for the youth who use them as places for information and for making "true friendships" (Herdt and Boxer, 1993; Greeley, 1994; Bennett, 1992).

Another theme that presents itself here is the prevalence of derogatory terms for gay and lesbian people in Catholic high schools. I wonder if there would not be more public outcry if words such as "nigger" and "spic" were as common in Catholic schools as "queer" and "fag." Some of those I interviewed didn't feel that the use of these words by their peers was meant to be taken literally. "Fag" was just something you called someone; it didn't mean you really were accusing someone of being gay. On the other hand, some of the people I interviewed did feel it was an accusation when it was used by their peers. When I interviewed counselors working in Catholic high schools, they acknowledged the prevalence of such terms as insults in their schools. Those working in all-boys schools frequently stated that "fag" was "the worst put-down you could give a guy in school." The counselors also questioned how literally these terms were meant when they were used. A few schools had policies punishing students who used these words in their schools. These policies seemed to be very effective in reducing name calling.

What are the attitudes of students in Catholic education toward derogatory words for gay and lesbian people? In my survey studies, one item, "Words such as 'fag' and 'dyke' as well as jokes about gay and lesbian people are not acceptable," gives some insight. In my 1990 study of high school Confirmation candidates in the Kansas City–St. Joseph Diocese, the responses to this item are disturbing: only 21.6 percent of males agreed with the statement as well as only 52.5 percent of females. My 1995 study of incoming freshman at a Catholic university shows some improvement; in this study, 46.9 percent of males and 92.9 percent of females agreed with the statement.

Mark's story cites the most extreme example of social dis-integration, antigay violence. The death of Matthew Shepard on a fence in Wyoming in 1998 certainly brought attention to this in our country. Unfortunately, Matthew Shepard and Mark are not isolated examples. Another person I interviewed, Nick (Chapter 6), also was physically assaulted in his Catholic high school. One also does not have to be the victim of anti-gay violence to be affected by it: Larry mentioned knowing one openly gay person in high school who people wanted to beat up. Becky (Chapter 2) noted that seeing a gay student beat up regularly by fellow students influenced her not to come out in high school.

The survey studies again give some insight into the attitudes of students in Catholic education toward antigay violence. The item here is, "Physical violence against gay and lesbian people is not acceptable." The 1990 study of Confirmation candidates shows a great problem with males; only 62.8 percent of males agreed with this statement. This number was much higher in the 1995 Catholic university freshman study, but still only 84.4 percent of males agreed with the statement. Clearly, a problem exists in the attitudes of our male students about antigay violence.

Other studies have shown that gay and lesbian youth are frequent targets of violence in high schools (Friend, 1993; Kissen, 1991; The Child Welfare League of America, 1991; The National Gay Task Force, 1984; Massachusetts Governor's Commission on Gay and Lesbian Youth, 1993). One study found that teachers as well as students have been reported to verbally harass gay and lesbian students. Such harassment often results in students dropping out of school (Witlock and Kamel, 1989). In a study published by the U.S. Department of Justice, Finn and McNeil (1987) found that gay and lesbian people are probably the most frequent victims of hate violence. Bohn (1985) reported that gay males are more frequently the victims of antigay violence than lesbians. Violence affects 20 to 40 percent of gay males. The overwhelming number of rapes perpetrated on men are committed by straight men against gay men. Victims of antigay violence are less likely to know their assailants than victims of other violent crimes; attacks tend to be more violent and involve larger numbers of assailants. Vergara (1985) found that gay and lesbian youth who have run away from home experience a number of difficulties in residential shelters, including gang rape by other residents. Hunter (1990) found that once gay and lesbian youth experience violence, a cycle begins where they perpetuate violence on themselves; youth who have been the victims of antigay violence are much more likely to consider and attempt suicide. The issue of antigay violence is very serious and cannot be ignored by Catholic schools.

Antigay violence is only the most dramatic example of the larger problem that has been the topic of this chapter. Catholic high schools are meant to be communities. Some of the students in these schools, however, are not part of the community. Gay and lesbian youth do not feel that they fit in with their peers in many cases. These students are not integrated into the community; rather, they spend their high school years dis-integrated from it.

Chapter 4

Institutional Dis-Integration

Educationally, homosexuality cannot and ought not to be skirted or ignored. The topic "must be faced in all objectivity by the pupil and the educator when the case presents itself" (Vatican Congregation for Catholic Education, 1983, article 101). First and foremost, we support modeling and teaching respect for every human person, regardless of sexual orientation.

United States Catholic Conference, 1991 (p. 56)

They're out there. You have homosexual students in your school. They're probably hiding. You need to address some small part of the curriculum to them. You know, you're supposed to be older than the students. Don't imitate their behavior.

Kevin

The Church's magisterium has frequently used the theme of integration to describe the purposes and functions of Catholic schools. Culture, science, faith, and students' lives are to be integrated into a whole in Catholic schools. The Vatican Congregation for Catholic Education has defined the school as "a privileged place in which, through a living encounter with a cultural inheritance, integral formation occurs" (1977, article 26). The congregation went on to state, "The specific mission of the school, then, is a critical, systematic transmission of culture in the light of faith and the bringing forth of the power of Christian virtue by the integration of culture with faith and of faith with living" (1977, article 49). All academic studies are to lead the student to God (1977, articles 39-42). The congregation stated in 1988 that Catholic schools have an educational philosophy of harmony between faith, culture, and life (The Vatican Congregation for Catholic Education, 1988, article 36). "There can be no conflict between faith and true scientific knowledge; both find their source in God" (The Vatican Congregation for Catholic Education, 1988, article 54).

This integration of the curriculum is expected to include sex education. The American bishops asserted, "The content of sex education embraces knowledge, values, science and religious belief" (United States Catholic Conference, 1981, p. 65). They recommended that sex education be integrated into other content areas and classes. Sex education is a right of every child, and parental opposition to all forms of sex education is in conflict with the teaching of the Church (United States Catholic Conference, 1968, 1972, 1979, 1981, 1991; Vatican Congregation for Catholic Education, 1983; Second Vatican Council, 1965). While chastity is the aim of Catholic sex education, forgiveness must be emphasized (United States Catholic Conference, 1991). Sexuality must be presented to students as a gift from God (United States Catholic Conference, 1981 and 1991; Vatican Congregation for Catholic Education, 1983). The American bishops have pointed out prudence, or "the ability to practice sound judgment in practical matters," as a needed characteristic in Catholic sex educators (United States Catholic Conference, 1991, p. 24). Pope John Paul II (1979) called for better sex education for Catholic youth. The Vatican Congregation for Catholic Education (1983) has stated that sex education is part of the Church's mission and is a mission of Catholic schools.

Surprisingly to some people, the Catholic magisterium has clearly stated that the topic of homosexuality is to be presented in Catholic education. At all levels, the magisterium has emphasized that acceptance of homosexual acts cannot be taught. At the same time, the topic is to be presented honestly, and acceptance of gay and lesbian people is to be taught. The Vatican Congregation for Catholic Education instructs those working in Catholic education that they must welcome gay and lesbian students (1983, articles 101-103). The American bishops instruct that the topic of homosexuality should be addressed in schools with students as young as age twelve and in the home by parents with children as young as age nine (United States Catholic Conference, 1981). In 1979, the USCC stated that gay and lesbian people should have special groups provided by the Church: "The aim should be to help them overcome the obstacles they face and achieve as much integration as they can into the larger community of faith" (United States Catholic Conference, article 196). In 1981, the USCC again called on the Catholic community to accept gay and lesbian people: "The person who is ostracized in his/her own Church community because of a homosexual orientation finds little comfort that the Church distinguishes between homosexual orientation and homosexual activity" (United States Catholic Conference, p. 40). The most extensive statement on the topic of homosexuality in Catholic education comes from the American bishops in 1991 and is presented in Appendix A. In this statement, the bishops insist that respect for the person is the primary message to be communicated to students. Also, those working with youth must accept that some of them are struggling to accept themselves as gay or lesbian people. In their 1997 statement to parents of gay and lesbian people (also in Appendix A), the American bishops' Committee on Marriage and Family insists that ministers of the Church must discuss homosexuality, must support gay and lesbian people and their families, and must educate themselves.

The American bishops have expressed a concern that doctrinal content be presented in whole (United States Catholic Conference, 1979, article 47). Do Catholic high schools present the whole message of the Church regarding the dignity and worth of gay and lesbian people, or do they present only the Church's condemnations of homosexual activity? Do Catholic high schools present any message at all, or are they silent on the topic? For gay and lesbian students, are their lives integrated with the culture and the faith through their experiences at Catholic high schools? Are they themselves integrated into the schools as institutions? I have chosen the following three stories to try to answer some of these questions. In Chapter 3, I discussed gay and lesbian students' dis-integration in Catholic high schools *socially;* in this chapter, I focus on their dis-integration in Catholic high schools *institutionally.*

PATTY

Patty attended a Catholic, coeducational high school in a rural area. The school was a cooperative effort of area parishes and served about 600 students. She attended all four years there and graduated in 1987. She described the school as homogenous religiously and ethnically.

Patty found the environment at her high school stifling. She said that the local town—a small, homogenous, Catholic settlement—reflected the school. Also, wealth played a role in determining student social groups. Religion was emphasized as the most important element, followed by sports. Patty did find some refreshing teachers who were willing to discuss more issues openly. She also liked theater. "The people in theater tended to be more open."

A major problem that Patty faced was the narrow and closed presentation of religion in classes. One priest presented very closed points of view; homosexuality was discussed in his class. "It was pretty much the worst thing you could possibly be or do against God. I mean, I remember it being emphasized that it was worse sometimes than murder or things like that." The discussion of homosexuality was limited in her high school experience to one presentation in religion class and to one English teacher who made snide remarks about Gertrude Stein.

The practice of religion through clubs, Masses, reconciliation services, and retreats was also difficult for Patty. She especially didn't like feeling forced to participate. "They felt a little uncomfortable because they were pretty much forced. It was noticeable if you didn't go to Communion at Mass or something. You actually got called on it by someone. I was having some questions anyway about Catholicism, and I just felt like there wasn't any room to express those. And I felt like being forced to do these things, that just made it worse for me. At the annual retreats, they were pretty much trying to explore your beliefs and things like that. I felt like I couldn't really say what I wanted to say about my beliefs. In the pro-life club, we just weren't taught any alternatives. We were brainwashed. Kids would think, 'This is the only way to think.'"

The pressure of these feelings became very difficult for Patty. "Internally, I'd say it created a lot of confusion, a lot of anger also. I went through the motions of the Mass and the reconciliation services, Pro-life Club, and that stuff. I went and did them, but inside I was feeling like, 'Why am I doing this?' and kind of angry. But I would participate, up until my senior year when I started to say, 'I don't really believe this.' So I felt a little stronger by that point."

Patty had an after-school job at a local pizza restaurant. It was there that she had experiences that made her examine her sexual identity more closely. "I'd say I was minimally aware. I knew I wasn't attracted to men, but I had no idea why. I don't think I ever heard the word 'lesbian' until maybe late my senior year. I just knew something wasn't clicking with me. I had a lot of first dates with guys. I didn't want to get any more involved by going steady with any of them." Patty did experience attraction to her female best friend. She remembered noticing how beautiful her friend looked at the prom when they double-dated. "I guess I was scared of those feelings. I just thought, 'That's stupid; that's bad. Who knows why you would have thought that. You just haven't met the right guy.' Rationalization."

Some students who were co-workers began to accuse Patty of being a lesbian because she became friends with a woman who worked at the restaurant who was a lesbian. "They picked it out before I did." When one boy at work asked her on a date and she declined, he began spreading rumors about her. "It was like the first time I'd heard the word. It scared me to death. I said, 'No! That's not me. That's just not me.' I really didn't think about it past that."

The images that Patty had of homosexuals were mostly stereotypes of gay men that came from movies or peers; stereotypes of cross-gender behavior were the strongest images she had. One male student in her school acted effeminate; students often made fun of him.

I asked Patty what her impressions were from the lesbian woman she knew at work. "She was just so much like me that I didn't think she was a lesbian. I just thought a lesbian would be somebody totally different, just totally beyond my experience. I had no idea what it would look like or anything. I thought she had a close and different relationship with this other woman, but I didn't want to explore that maybe this is me, and maybe that's part of my attraction to her as my friend. I didn't even want to get into that. I felt like it would be the scariest thing in the world to be. I couldn't even imagine what that would be like."

Patty did eventually self-identify as a lesbian over Christmas break in her first year of college. At that time, she had a sexual experience with another woman. She also met many more lesbian women in college. She believes that coming out is different for men than for women, and gay men are more likely to know they are gay and act on it sooner than lesbian women.

"In high school, it would have been helpful to have met adult lesbians so that I could better understand what that meant. If the Church could just be a little more accepting of the reality of people's lives on so many topics—birth control, women priests, lesbians, and gays."

KEVIN

Kevin graduated from high school in 1994. He attended all four years at a Catholic, all-boys school run by a men's religious order in the suburbs. There were over 900 students at his school. Kevin had come out to himself only recently, four months before my interviews with him. He had some incredible insights into the culture of his high school.

Kevin was harassed by his classmates for being gay, which was very confusing for him because he did not yet identify himself as gay in high school. "Freshman year, I did have a reputation of being a homosexual. I don't know why, because I didn't act like one. By senior year, I had completely quelled it and removed any doubt from anyone's mind that I was heterosexual, with the exception of a few people who I think just teased me to irk me, not because they actually thought I was." Kevin described to me his reactions to peer harassment. "By the end of my sophomore year, I had learned to defend myself, not in a physical sense but in a verbal sense. I could tear somebody apart just as fast as they could tear me apart."

In the locker room, without a teacher around, Kevin was harassed by his fellow students a great deal during his freshman year. He was ridiculed for being unathletic, and he was teased for being gay. "One guy would come up to me and act like a drag queen. He would come up to me and say [affecting a lisp], 'Oh, you look so sexy today.

Would you like to blow me?'" The locker room was a place of extreme anxiety for Kevin. "Some people probably would say, 'If you're gay, you probably loved the locker room in high school because you got to stare at all those guys.' *No,* you don't! It was threatening as hell because what happens if you get turned on or you get excited? Then people *will* know." He remembered one boy who got an erection in the showers; he was tormented for weeks by his classmates until someone saw him on a date with his girlfriend.

Kevin noted that this harassment was worse in his earlier years at school. "Freshman are cruel beings; so are sophomores. Juniors tend to be a little more like adults, and by senior year people tend to come to the point where they've accepted your difference. Maybe not in a nurturing way of acceptance, but acceptance in the way that they realize that harassing you isn't going to change you, and they're stuck with you as you are. They can either live with that and like it, or they can just not associate with you." At his senior retreat, one student apologized for harassing him in earlier grades. This was very important to Kevin; he felt that he bonded with his class on the retreat.

Kevin seemed to make a conscious effort to "act straight." This seemed to mostly come out through pressure to date girls. "If all the other guys were commenting about a girl's breasts, I would too—or her legs. I achieved acting straight partly through convincing myself. If you're going to play the part and *act* like a heterosexual, you better sure as hell convince *yourself* you're a heterosexual. So I dated several girls in high school. I never really went very far with any of them, partly because the interest was not there, not at the drive part. The interest was there in proving to my friends that I was heterosexual. Just getting to the point with a girl that if she had a day off of school, she would come over to my school. I could sit there outside the school and do a little kissing or something just to prove to people that I was heterosexual." Kevin was sometimes confused by the interest his classmates had in girls. "'Why are they so concerned about the size of her breasts? Why are they so interested?' Because, honestly, in my mind, I didn't understand."

Kevin's peers had very negative and stereotypical impressions of gay and lesbian people, views which Kevin shared. "Someone who talked with a lisp, who was a little feminine. Part of the reason why I couldn't identify with being gay was because I wasn't feminine. I did not have this view of a diverse gay community where you've got everything from the one hundred percent U.S. American man USDA choice to the real effeminate drag queen who's practically a woman. All my peers thought being gay, or being a faggot, was being effeminate. They'd crack jokes and would 'act gay,' put on this lisp, talk like a girl. And that was acting like a fag. To be honest, I had this negative view of the morals of the gay community because that is what the gay community is portrayed as. They are portrayed as people who sleep around and all that. That was probably one of the psychological reasons that I couldn't identify with the gay community."

Homosexuality was rarely addressed in the school curriculum. "I can think of maybe once or twice that it came up. It was always based on the principle of equality, 'They're human beings too, and you should leave them alone, not make fun of them.' That was the only thing. But there was never any talk about what it was like to be one, or how you would know if you were one. Not even any of the diversity stuff like, 'Just because you're gay doesn't mean you're effeminate.' There was none of that. That would have been helpful for me. I think the administration was pretty conservative and would have stopped any teacher who was going to do that for fear of complaints from parents. Parents sent their kids to Catholic schools to protect them from liberalism. It would have been helpful for me to hear some of that stuff from a real person. All the information I got was from encyclopedias or books I would sneak in the library."

I found it very interesting that a person so observant and articulate as Kevin still had difficulty defining himself as gay in high school. "Despite the fact that I had a lot of homosexual activity in eighth grade and freshman year, I never *thought* I was a homosexual. I always thought it was just a phase I was going through. I even looked it up in encyclopedias and psychology books about adolescents having homosexual experiences and that was okay and to a certain extent normal. So, I passed myself off more, in my mind." Kevin actually became more convinced in later high school years that he was straight by forcing himself to date girls, and also because he experienced less gay teasing from his peers. "All through high school, I spent so much time watching other guys. And at the same time, I would tell myself, 'I am a heterosexual. I'm just giving into my phase again.' It was a really weird internal sort of thing going on inside my head. I would imagine doing something with a male, and within the same thought, the very next thought would be, 'What am I doing with Kelly this Friday night?' And I just passed it off as a phase, and 'I should just forget about that. That isn't me.' " Kevin found these thoughts threatening. "Despite the fact that in your head it's what you always fantasize about, in real life it's, 'I might be found out,' or, 'Would I really, *really* want this to happen? If it did happen, then that would mean that I really am a homosexual, and I'm not. I'm *not!*' I thought, 'Maybe when I get farther with a girl, I'll enjoy that more, and these thoughts will leave my head.' "

Kevin had some of the most astute observations on the values and culture of his school of all the interviewees. What is fascinating to me is the way the students' values interacted with the curriculum. "To be a jock was cool; to be smart was not, even to the point that some people who were smart would pretend not to be smart just to be cool. In general, organizations were for intellectuals, not cool people. Surprisingly, theater was safe. It was safe because you could meet chicks in theater. By senior year, it was safe to be in theater, and some of the jocks, in fact, were in theater. Freshman year, it was not cool to be in theater because that meant you were a fag. Film appreciation was cool because you got to watch movies. Band was cool because you got to play rock music. Mass became cool because one teacher had a rock band, and he used to play U2 music at Mass, and one priest used to cuss in his homilies. A religious service club was bad until they started doing it with one of the girls' schools. Then it became okay because you could meet chicks. Model UN became cool because you got out of school for a day and you could meet chicks. Newspaper was safe because you wrote about sports. Yearbook was for fags. Students who wrote for newspaper were treated differently than students who wrote for the yearbook. Teachers who advised newspaper were treated differently than teachers who advised for yearbook. This was true for all the clubs; advisors for cool things were cool. Advisers for nerd things were nerds. They were viewed as geeks because they were nurturing and caring versus the coaches who rode their students. Sports recognition was public and informal. Academic recognition was: you got a pin at a ceremony. The school gave athletes cool recognition, and they gave nerds nerdy recognition." Kevin cut a few sections from sports in the yearbook when he was the editor. "It was my little way of saying, 'I'm important too.'"

Kevin viewed these attitudes toward the curriculum as coming from a much deeper set of values. "Values were not allowed in general. To be critical, that was okay. To actually care about something, that was unmanly. Caring was feminine. Giving a shit was feminine, in the sense that, you know, 'I'm a male. I'm cool. I don't need anybody or anything. I am completely independent, and I'll be damned if I'm going to lift a finger for anything or anybody unless I get some immediate gratification out of it.' It was a fine, fine line where if you could justify in some way using the set of adolescent values of rock music, sports, sex, women, if there was something from that culture that you could mix with one of the intellectual things, it would be okay. If you couldn't, it was wrong."

Kevin believed P. E. classes should have been tracked just like academic classes. "Putting me in a class with people who can run ten times faster than me isn't going to do anything for my self-esteem or my ability because I'm not going to work for something that I can't achieve."

"The big feminine thing, though, was religion. That was considered a feministic thing. That was something the girls in the girls' schools did. In the mind of an adolescent, if you think religion is okay, you're acting like one of the girls over there. To reveal religious sentiment or personal feelings, that was uncool, was really feministic." At his sophomore retreat, Kevin's peers harassed him because he participated in a religious small group discussion. The harassment was due in part to the fact that it was religion, a taboo in the area of peer values; it was also because the new campus minister who led the retreat was considered to be gay by the students because he spoke with a lisp and because he was "touchy-feely." "The mere fact that I even participated in an exercise he was running, combined with just the whole idea of caring about my religion, that was wrong." Kevin liked this teacher very much, and felt valued by him. "He was someone I could talk to." He also believed this teacher was experiencing many of the same trials that he was. The teacher began teaching at Kevin's high school during his freshman year.

Kevin had some advice for teachers. "They're out there. You have homosexual students in your school. They're probably hiding. You need to address some small part of the curriculum to them. You know, you're supposed to be older than the students. *Don't* imitate their behavior." One teacher at his school used the word "faggot." One of the coaches called the students "ladies."

Kevin saw his struggle with accepting his sexuality as a struggle with identity. "Everyone is given the self-concept that they are heterosexual. From birth on, you are told that you're going to meet a member of the opposite sex, and you're going to fall in love, and you're going to have a house of your own, and you're going to have children and live happily ever after. When you're gay, this gives you a self-concept struggle."

Kevin felt very conflicted over issues of homosexuality and Catholicism. He acknowledged that he never was exposed to the Church's condemnations of homosexual behavior. He was disturbed by the writings of St. Paul in the Bible over the topic. "Well, maybe he's right. Maybe God is telling me that I shouldn't be homosexual. Well, screw that! Because my hormones are telling me something else, and if I end up in Hell, well, I really couldn't do anything about it. Maybe that's not a healthy view, but that's how I feel." He had become angry with Church leadership over its teachings on homosexuality. "Catholic leaders could show some more compassion demonstrated publicly. It would make being a Catholic homosexual a lot easier. I put a lot of stake in that area of my life, and to have a conflict about whether I was a homosexual or not, and then to put a faith conflict in that, it just made it so much harder. In my mind, it was just another reason why I couldn't identify with this whole homosexual thing because not only did it mean that I would have to act like a woman, it would also mean that I would have to leave the Catholic Church. I wouldn't have a faith life. I'd be sinning. And I wouldn't believe in Christ or something like that. And I'd go to Hell or something like that. I never had a teacher say this, but it's still in the Church. It's not so much condemned but not shown acceptance. Maybe there were some religion teachers who showed it equality, but it wasn't a nurturing equality. It wasn't, 'This is okay.' It was, 'They're human beings too, so let them do their thing.' It wasn't the warm, nurturing equality. It was more of a begrudged equality."

ALICE

Alice graduated in 1981. She attended a very exclusive Catholic girls' high school run by a women's religious order. The school was located in an affluent suburban area, with about half of the approximately 200 students boarded on campus. Much of Alice's experience with the school was shaped by the fact that she was not Catholic and did not come from a family background similar to that of most other students; her mother was divorced and worked two jobs to afford the school's tuition and to raise her seven children. Although Alice never caused any discipline problems in school, her younger sister did.

Alice had attended public schools through the end of sixth grade. Her mother felt that the local public schools were not preparing her well enough academically. Her mother then sent Alice for one year to a private school that emphasized academics exclusively. After dissatisfaction with this, her mother enrolled her for eighth grade in the coeducational grade school associated with her future high school.

The school had a fairly large international population. Most international students were from Latin America, but there were also students from Asia, Europe, and daughters of Americans living overseas. Alice also described some of the girls as "bad girls" whose parents had sent them to boarding school to be supervised. The school had a few Jewish students, some African-American Baptist students, and Asian students, most of whom were not Catholic. "There was this big 'Are you Catholic? Are you not?' thing going on." Alice was raised with no religion until her mother decided to have her and her siblings baptized as Episcopalians during her senior year of high school. There was no follow-up in practice after this, however. Alice did enjoy the school's Catholic Masses. "They were very student involved, very social, very loving, very caring. Those were positive times for me. I knew enough from religion class to know what it meant to take Communion. I didn't really believe in the Catholic faith, so I didn't take Communion. But I was involved in everything. I played music in the Masses. I still believe that a lot of those girls were just going through the motions at the Masses."

Alice was very involved in the social life of the school. She served on student council, and the other students on the council were most of her friends in high school. "I was a pretty reliable-dependable-type person. Having something for which I felt responsible gave me self-confidence. I knew that I could do things, that I could get things done. Feeling good about myself helped give me a sense of belonging at the school." While she said she was not "cool" in high school, she was still popular.

Alice liked her high school for most of her time there. She had skipped a grade in elementary school, thus she was a year and a half younger than most of the people in her class. She described herself as "immature" and believed that her school was much easier for her than a public high school would have been.

Not having the same affluence did at times set her apart from some of the other girls. She wore used uniforms rather than new ones. She answered the phone at the front desk after school, which indicated that she was on scholarship. The greatest difference in affluence was living off campus; this separated many of the very affluent students from the day students. "The dorms always looked fun and interesting, and I wanted to be a part of that. But when I would go there, I felt alienated and felt like I didn't fit in. Some of that was money, and some of that was, 'You're day students. You don't fit in here.'" Some students talked about shopping and dressing up on the weekends while Alice had to work on weekends. Overall, however, she said the school environment was noncompetitive between students. Differences were very subtle.

Alice liked the fact that the structure of her school reduced the pressure for her to date. The school would "import" buses of boys from a Catholic boys' school for dances. She also went to dances with dates that either her mother or friends arranged for her. When she went on other dates, it was usually with a group of friends from the public high school. She met boys at Model UN and through the mixers arranged by the school. Although she did begin to wish she had a boyfriend in her later years of high school, it was not a strong desire. She liked that the lack of dating pressure reduced a variety of concerns, such as worrying too much about appearance at school.

Although Alice appreciated the safety of her high school, she did somewhat resent that it did not prepare her socially for the real world. Her freshman year of college was difficult for her. She was shocked by the heavy drinking and kick-off toga party in her dorm the first week, and she wound up crying on the phone to her mother. She didn't know how to handle the environment, and was viewed as a nerd by other college students.

Alice was introverted in high school, but she did have very close friendships with some other girls. She described her best friend, Betty as "someone I could confide in." She was also very close to Jenny, who she thought of as her "big sister." The high school had juniors and seniors mentor incoming freshman. "I'd have to say, somewhat retrospectively, that I had a major crush on this woman. Her graduation was really hard for me. I remember thinking, 'If I were a guy, I'd go out with her. She would be such a good girlfriend.' It was really in my head."

She saw the all-female composition of the school as very safe and comfortable for her. "There were very few male teachers and just an occasional priest on campus. There was a lot of closeness. There wasn't a lot of competition. Uniforms helped with that too; you couldn't doll yourself up a lot because you had to meet the dress code. There was a lot of physical closeness. We would walk around campus with our arms over each others' shoulders, like totally normal. We never even thought about it. I think it was just good for me, being comfortable with those physical expressions of caring. A lot of my friends, they just never were like that. They went to public high schools where you would be murdered if you did something like that. I don't think we could have done that if we were at a coed school or a public school."

When girls from other schools came on campus for sporting events, they had very different reactions to this closeness between the students. "These other girls would see two girls walking by arm in arm and be like, 'Oh man! These guys are all lesbos!' And we were not totally sure what that meant, but we knew it was like a female thing. We would just play it up even more because we thought it was hysterical! I think we had just a very murky idea of what that meant."

Alice lacked any clear images of lesbians as an adolescent. Her mother had gay male friends who were hairdressers. Her mother would go out to gay clubs with some of these friends in a group which included other straight women, but lesbians were never mentioned by her mother, and no other images were presented for Alice. "I never knew a lesbian. I was never exposed to that. 'Gay' meant gay men. It was a male thing." Gay men were never seen as something scary for

Alice when she was in high school. They were more something entertaining, and in a sense like a circus show. "They were exotic and harmless."

Homosexuality was never discussed in the school and homosexual images were never presented. In fact, there was no sex education. Alice did take a religion class, "Marriage and Family." In this class, relationships were discussed, but sex education was never taught. Alice's mother bought her some books to be used for sex education at home.

Alice was attracted to some girls at school, but did not connect this with her sexual identity. "There were some girls I was really enamored with, but I wanted to be their sister. It was really coming from more of an emotional place for me, not a sexual place. I would call it now, 'I love this person. I want to be around this person so much.' I don't think those were words I could have even used then. I remember those feelings, but they were not sexual; they were emotional. It never occurred to me to be sexual with these girls I was attracted to. That never crossed my mind." Alice saw this as a difference between lesbians and gay men in coming out. Alice did not understand herself as a lesbian until she became sexually involved with another female student when she was in college. She was grateful that she wasn't more aware in high school. She saw that this could be an incredible burden for some teenagers, and she felt that it was best for most gay and lesbian teenagers not to come out to their peers in high school.

Alice identified strongly with some faculty and staff of the school. One was the school counselor. "She was your proverbial 'warm fuzzy' person, and she was like a magnet. People really hung on her. Pretty much everyone was in her office at some time. She had a big influence on me." Alice viewed her adult career as a counselor as closely related to her positive experiences with her own school counselor. Alice also felt supported by her music teacher because this woman had a Mormon background, to which Alice could relate. "She had a value system that I felt I needed some support with at that time, like not smoking, no drinking, no wild sex. That wasn't my nature anyway, but a lot of people were getting into that kind of stuff, and she really supported me in not having to do those kinds of things. I really appreciated that." Her Spanish teacher also expressed a great deal of "unconditional positive regard" toward Alice.

Alice described all of these women as "mothering." When I asked her if they were somehow taking on a mother role for her in place of her own mother, she responded, "Not so much a mothering thing as a second parent. On some levels, I may have been compensating for a lack of time with my own mother, but it was more like an additional person to talk to. Sort of an authority figure who could hear anything and, because you weren't *their* kid, they weren't going to freak out. I think that all three of them acted as mentors in a way, and that was something I needed outside the home as I began to individuate from my mother."

Alice's great problem in school resulted from her poor relationship with the administration. She was very angry with the principal, one of the sisters. "She was two-faced, condescending, and untrustworthy. I think she had a major problem with the fact that I was not Catholic, the fact that my mother was divorced, and, related to that, the fact that we didn't have a whole lot of money. We were probably lower-middle class. We were just not the picturesque mom-and-pop-and-kids family that had, like, twelve hundred kids. She didn't like that from the get-go. Now, I was a really good student and a student leader, so she had to sort of overcome herself. Now, my sister didn't have quite as nice of a trail behind her, and I think that caused a lot of problems."

Every senior met with the principal to discuss college plans. The principal discouraged Alice from applying to expensive schools, which she took as a put-down. Alice acknowledged that her family situation was different, and it did show itself at times in the school. Her mother could not attend many of the mother-daughter teas because she was working; her older brother came for father-daughter day at the school. Very few students at the school had divorced parents.

Alice worked at the front desk of the administration building where the student records were kept. A friend suggested to her that she should look up her own record, which she did. "I was horrified to see notes that the principal had written, like personal things about me, mostly about my mother. Things like not having enough money, things that weren't true! We were not super wealthy, but we were fine. I was also upset to see things there I had told my Spanish teacher. These were not awful things—typical adolescent stuff, like wondering about college. It was like a double-whammy because I lost all trust in my Spanish teacher and all respect for my school." She told her mother what she had done and what she had found; her mother then asked her to look up her sister's file. She found even worse things in there. "Confidentiality just did not exist, and I felt very judged. I loved my high school, and everything I had loved about my high school just felt dirty after that." It also began to form her understanding of what a system was. "If you do something in one part of it, it shows up in another part." She reacted by "really pulling in and not telling anyone much of anything that was going on with me." Alice said that it enhanced privacy issues for the rest of her life, which also shaped her profession as a counselor.

Her discovery of the student files came just six weeks before graduation. It was only the foreshadowing of a much larger disappointment. The school gave out one award, considered to be the most honorable, to one senior every year. "Everyone I knew said that I would get that award, and I kept saying, 'I don't think so. I'm not Catholic; I just don't have the right family background; my sister has caused all sorts of problems this year.' A staff person—she wanted me to be prepared, so she told me that I wasn't going to get the award, and she told me why [because her family was not wealthy and her mother was single]. They wound up giving the award to someone who, it turns out, failed a number of her tests at the end. They gave me another award. I didn't really care by then, but I did feel judged. But what makes me angry to this very day is that if you're going to accept people into your school, then you need to accept them totally from whatever background."

Graduation was difficult for Alice. "It was just kind of a bittersweet end, because I *was* my high school. That was my life. I *loved* my school. I *loved* it. I was, like, there all the time. It was really a perfect place for me, and then it was like discovering Watergate when you think the government is perfect. I think I really went through a huge realization. 'Oh, this really isn't as idyllic behind the scenes as I thought it was.' At graduation, I was like, 'Thank God I'm getting out of here.'" She was embarrassed to say that she was still bothered about not receiving the award, but admitted that it had a great impact on her. "It just really bothered me that they set up one set of standards and then didn't follow them. The fact that these were nuns, were religious, that made it even worse."

REFLECTIONS

I selected the previous three stories to illustrate some of the ways in which the gay and lesbian people whom I interviewed felt dis-integrated from their schools as institutions. The strongest way in which this was seen cannot be discussed at length because it concerns something that was missing. Most of the people I interviewed said that homosexuality was never discussed in the formal curriculum of their Catholic high schools. In a few cases, the topic was brought up by a student. Bob (Chapter 5) told me that a girl in his high school gave a report on homosexuality for a class. When she was in high school, Gina (Chapter 2) gave such a report. In the few cases in which the interviewees indicated that the topic was brought up by school staff, it was usually brief but did focus on the rights of gay and lesbian people. Some exceptions occurred when faculty and staff made negative comments on homosexuality, but this will be discussed in Chapter 5.

The silence of high schools on the topic of homosexuality has been the concern of some researchers. Friend (1993) and Witlock and Kamel (1989) point out that high schools systematically include heterosexuality and systematically exclude homosexuality. Most school libraries lack any material on the topic. Faculty often make gay jokes. Homosexuality often is only presented in the curriculum in the context of AIDS, making it appear to be a dangerous behavior. Teachers are afraid to introduce the topic because they may be harassed. Kielwasser and Wolf (1991, 1992) have argued that the lack of gay and lesbian youth presented on television represents a symbolic "annihilation" of this population that contributes to their sense of isolation and creates a "spiral of silence," which is reflected in the high school curriculum.

Almost all of the counselors I interviewed agreed that homosexuality was rarely or never presented in the curricula at their schools. There were a few exceptions. Ms. Brown, a counselor and teacher at her suburban, coeducational, Catholic high school for fourteen years, with seven years previous experience at two other Catholic high schools, included the topic in presentations she gave in classes on dating and sexuality. Ms. Zwick had been a counselor at her suburban, coeducational, diocesan school for twenty-nine years and previously a teacher at the school for five years. In the senior religion classes at her school, gays and lesbians had been invited to come and talk to the classes. Also, gay and lesbian teachers were "out" to the other faculty. She also felt that the school's policy of allowing students to bring a friend of any sex to dances rather than requiring a date was helpful. Ms. Edwards had been a counselor for nine years at her suburban, all-girls school run by a women's order. Two years prior to the interview, Ms. Edwards noted that an openly lesbian student had been elected by her class as the prom queen. This was not meant as a joke by the students, but was basically a popularity contest, as in other elections. The prom queen brought another girl as her escort to the dance, and the couple had their picture in the yearbook. Some division occurred in Ms. Edwards' school's faculty and staff over this, with the older faculty, the "very Catholic" faculty, and some of the nuns expressing opposition. It does demonstrate, however, that progress can occur in policies at Catholic schools.

Interestingly, my 1995 survey of Catholic university freshmen showed that students graduating from Catholic high schools had more positive attitudes toward gay and lesbian people and homosexuality than students graduating from non-Catholic high schools. Although this surprised some of the counselors I interviewed, others felt that it was caused by the emphasis on justice education in Catholic schools; a transfer had taken place from justice topics usually discussed to the topic of gay and lesbian people. Some believed that although Catholic schools make very little mention of homosexuality, it is still more than the topic is discussed in public high schools. It is worth noting that although the gay and lesbian alumni who I interviewed felt that the topic of homosexuality should be included in the curriculum of Catholic high schools, they also felt that it should be integrated with other justice issues in the curriculum. In a study of junior high students in Catholic schools, Forliti (1984) found that students in Catholic schools had a greater concern about social justice issues than students in public schools.

What role can the curriculum play in shaping attitudes about homosexuality? College undergraduates who have received sex education through a rational-emotional model which focused on identity, decision making, emotions, and relationships had more positive attitudes toward gay and lesbian people than those taught through traditional models focusing on pregnancy, sexually transmitted diseases, and physiological aspects of sex (Watter, 1985). In a study of Catholic high school seniors, Kline (1991) found that having a longer time spent in sex education in school increased students' knowledge and improved sexual attitudes. A number of studies have shown that young peoples' attitudes toward gays and lesbians can be improved through classroom activities such as discussions, videos, speaker panels, role-playing activities, and integration of the topic into the larger curriculum (Barbetta, 1989; Rudolph, 1988; Wool, 1987; Wells, 1989; McCleskey, 1991; Reinhardt, 1995; McClintock, 1992; Aitken, 1993; Serdahely and Ziemba, 1985). Salmi (1994) found that an educational program was effective in improving attitudes of students at a Catholic university. Studies have also shown that knowing a gay or lesbian person tends to improve an individual's attitudes toward homosexuality (Hansen, 1982; Grieger and Ponterotto, 1988; Millham, San Miguel, and Kellog, 1976).

At the level of higher education, Catholic schools have not always been friendly to their gay and lesbian students. The "Gay Rights Coalition" had to battle Georgetown University for almost a decade in courtrooms in order to be recognized by the university (Rullman, 1991). Some dioceses and seminaries implemented policies in the 1980s seeking to eliminate gay candidates from priesthood (Nugent, 1989).

The culture of high schools greatly affects how gay and lesbian students integrate with the school. Reed (1992, 1993, 1994) has found that gay and lesbian high school students experience school alone in a special way. The school is a sexualized environment specifically, heterosexualized; it punishes homosexuality, rewards heterosexuality, and affirms negative beliefs about homosexuality. Gay and lesbian students may perceive the sexualized nature of the school environment while other students as well as faculty and staff may not. Gay and lesbian students experience unique problems in their high schools: they are made to feel abnormal and are forced to choose between acceptance and honesty; they experience shame, guilt, and a conflict between alienation from the school and alienation from themselves. Mallon (1994) has also discovered that the pressure to conceal distorts almost all gay and lesbian student relationships and causes a sense of isolation.

The role of the teachers in the schools had a very strong effect on how safe the people who I interviewed felt. If students felt truly cared for by a teacher, that teacher was seen as helpful or safe by students. This seemed to be more important than personality, politics, or sexual identity. Some interviewees used parental terms for caring teachers, such as Alice and also Allen (Chapter 5). Teachers who were judgmental or who did not protect students were seen as very threatening. Recall that Mark (Chapter 3) was most angry about the teachers in his school not protecting him from the violence of his classmates. Alice's story of residual anger as an adult about the judgmental attitudes of her school's faculty and staff points to the depth of this impact upon individuals. Interestingly, Kevin reported feeling comfortable with a teacher who students thought was gay. With most of the people I interviewed, their reactions were the opposite. If they perceived a teacher as gay or lesbian, they avoided the teacher for fear of "guilt by association."

The role of gay and lesbian teachers needs some special attention. Friend (1993) has pointed out that closeted gay and lesbian teachers model closeting rather than pride to their students. In a study of gay and lesbian teachers, Kissen (1993) found that almost all of the teachers in her study experienced great strain in their personal lives because of the pressure to conceal. This is a difficult area to discuss. There are those who strongly advocate the need for gay and lesbian teachers to "come out of the closet." The need for gay and lesbian adult role models for gay and lesbian youth is very clear (Herdt and Boxer, 1993; Jennes, 1992). My interview study, however, does not confirm this. All employees in Catholic high schools need to discuss and examine this area more closely. Clearly, the rights and needs of gay and lesbian faculty must be taken into consideration as well as the needs of gay and lesbian students.

Kevin discussed the anxiety he experienced in the boys' locker room. This was a common problem for many of the men I interviewed; both locker rooms and bathrooms were very threatening. A good deal of this was the fear of sexual arousal, which Kevin has described and which was echoed by Tom (Chapter 1) and Nick (Chapter 6). Part of the problem was caused by the lack of adult supervision in these areas, thus allowing harassment by students.

One of the counselors I interviewed, Brother George, acknowledged that the locker room can be a very scary place for some male students. Brother George had been a counselor at his all-boys, urban-residential Catholic high school run by his order for eight years. He had served at the school for twenty years as administrator, teacher, or counselor. He had worked a total of five years teaching and counseling in three other all-boys, Catholic high schools. He stated that some potential students for his school did not attend because the school required swimming. As recently as ten years before my interview with him, students swam nude in the school. By the time of my interviews, they swam in small, athletic-style bathing suits, which still caused some students to feel self-conscious and uncomfortable.

Alice discussed at length the lack of confidentiality she experienced at her school. Fear of a lack of confidentiality prompted some of the people I interviewed to avoid the counseling services at their high schools, such as Gina (Chapter 2) and Bob (Chapter 5). In many cases, it simply did not occur to students that they could use the counseling services to talk about issues that involved their sexual identities. Tom (Chapter 1) noted that a neutral environment such as a counselor's office will not prompt a student to discuss a difficult issue such as homosexuality. The issue must be introduced by the counselor. In all fairness to high school counselors, I must point out that the people I interviewed typically did not discuss these issues with anyone. Although it was often the most pressing issue in their lives, for the most part they went through it alone.

The school counselors whom I interviewed were disturbed by this finding but also not surprised. Before our interview, Brother George had discussed some of the material I sent to him with his staff. With four counselors who had fifty-eight collective years of counseling among them, only once had a student come to one of them to talk about being homosexual, and that was in a public school. With the twelve counselors I interviewed, the highest rate of a student discussing homosexuality with them was once every three years. When students had discussed homosexuality with counselors, it was not usually the "presenting problem." The students came to discuss broader issues of fitting in or family problems. One counselor, Mr. Alberts, felt that it was important for school guidance counselors not to present themselves as just college-and-career-prep people. He had been a counselor at his coed, urban-residential, diocesan high school for three years, a high school counselor for sixteen years, and a teacher for five years. He had worked in four different Catholic high schools. Ms. Brown believed that the fear of "it getting out" prevented students from coming to talk to school counselors about homosexuality. "They're afraid that they would just be crucified if it ever got out, and they would be." Another counselor, Brother Peter, had valuable insight. He had worked as a counselor for three years at an inner-city, all-boys, Catholic high school run by his order; he had worked as a counselor and teacher for a total of twenty-four years before this at two other all-boys Catholic high schools and one coeducational Catholic high school. In the course of our interview, he realized that he tended to assume that all the students he counseled were straight. He would make conversation by asking them if they had girlfriends. He noted that possibly by not making this assumption and asking more open-ended questions, he could create the possibility for students to bring up homosexuality.

Other researchers have found that although high school counselors are open to working with gay and lesbian students, they often feel unprepared to do so (Hunt, 1993; Sears, 1988). Researchers have also found that workshops and special training can improve the abilities of counselors and teachers to work with gay and lesbian youth (Lipkin, 1992; Remafedi, 1993).

Some of the people I interviewed found religion to be a comforting subject for them. Alice expressed how much she loved the Masses at her school. Also, Gina (Chapter 2) and Allen (Chapter 5) found comfort in the religious aspects of their schooling. This was not the case for all the people I interviewed, as I will discuss in Chapter 5.

One theme, which came out very clearly in Kevin's story, was the prevalence of gender conformity in some Catholic high schools. This seemed to be a strong aspect of their school's culture, which contributed greatly to discomfort in many of the people I interviewed. Related to this was a pressure to date the opposite sex. Kevin and Patty felt that dating was a must, and many others whom I interviewed felt the same pressure. With the counselors I interviewed, those working in single-sex schools tended to see a greater pressure for students to conform to gender roles. Other researchers have found that people who have rigid attitudes regarding gender roles also tend to have negative attitudes toward homosexuality (Newman, 1985; Ellis, 1989; Bleich, 1989; Black and Stevenson, 1985; O'Neil, 1982, 1984).

Friend (1993) has argued that heterosexism and sexism in high schools are closely related. These two attitudes prevent non-sexual intimacy between friends of the same sex in high schools. DuVal (1991) did find that although in a particular Catholic high school male students' attitudes toward women were more negative than female students' attitudes, males were more likely to change their attitudes through a social justice curriculum. The American bishops have repeatedly stated that Catholic education must teach against sexism (United States Catholic Conference, 1972, 1981, 1990, 1991).

Another aspect of these schools as institutions deals with their compositions and locations. The gender makeup of the school had an impact on the reactions of the people I interviewed. Alice felt that her school was a safe place *because* it contained all girls. This was also true of Gina (Chapter 2) and Denise (Chapter 6), as well as a number of women I interviewed who attended all-girls schools. On the other hand, males who attended all-boys schools, such as Kevin, had the opposite reaction; their schools were worse places to be *because* they were all boys. Family affluence of students also seemed to break down community in many of these schools. This was reported by Patty in this chapter as well as by several interviewees in other chapters. Patty also pointed out a problem expressed by Sue (Chapter 3), Nick (Chapter 6) and Mark (Chapter 3): people who attended schools in rural areas tended to report greater levels of negative attitudes toward gay and lesbian people. All these factors seemed to contribute to school climate and shaped much of the experiences of the students there.

Some insights from counselors may be helpful here. Mr. Alberts felt the issues of affluence and single-sex schools were related because students who attended single-sex schools often came from more affluent families. For boys, these schools provide many important business connections later in life. Loss of social status through coming out would also mean a loss in future socioeconomic status for them. Brother George felt that the all-male environment of the school where he worked definitely contributed to a less tolerant atmosphere. "Here, in an all-boys school, it would be close to suicide to even bring up the topic for the students." Ms. Lewis was in her first year as a counselor at her all-girls, suburban Catholic high school. She had been a counselor at another all-girls Catholic school for four years and a teacher for nine years at another all-girls Catholic high school. She felt that the affluence of many of her students contributed to more conservative attitudes. It has been a concern of the Church's magisterium: Catholic schools must not become schools for only the wealthy (Vatican Congregation for Catholic Education, 1977).

My 1995 survey of Catholic university freshmen indicated that students graduating from coeducational Catholic high schools had more positive attitudes toward gay and lesbian people and homosexuality than those graduating from single-sex Catholic high schools. Counselors who worked in all-girls schools often questioned this finding for all-girls schools, although none were surprised about this result for all-boys schools. Although my sample was not large enough to distinguish between these two groups, a close examination of the data did not indicate any difference in this trend for female respondents versus male respondents. Although the people I interviewed who attended all-girls schools felt that their environments were safer than coeducational environments, the study does not indicate that attitudes of girls in these schools were better toward homosexuality.

Both the 1990 and the 1995 surveys clearly showed a difference between male and female responses. As I noted earlier in this chapter, research indicates that males tend to have more negative attitudes toward homosexuality and gay and lesbian people than females do (Herek, 1985b; Aguero, Bloch, and Byrne, 1985; Reinhardt, 1995; Kite, 1985; D'Augelli, 1989; D'Augelli and Rose, 1990; Newman, 1985; Hansen, 1982; Watter, 1985; Wells, 1989). None of the counselors I interviewed were surprised by this finding.

Geography has been found by some researchers to have an influence on people's attitudes about homosexuality (DeCrescenzo, 1985; Herek, 1985b). Although I cannot go into detail because it would compromise the confidentiality of the people I interviewed, I can say that my interviews with counselors demonstrated that schools in more liberal areas were much more progressive in how they included gay and lesbian topics in the curriculum and how they treated their gay and lesbian students.

Although Catholic high schools are meant to integrate "culture with faith and faith with living," this task does not seem to be accomplished with gay and lesbian students. The realities of their lives hit a wall of silence in most Catholic high schools. The cultures and structures of their schools do not invite them in but rather quietly (and probably most often unintentionally) keep them out. Their lives are not integrated in these institutions; they are dis-integrated from their schools instead.

Chapter 5

Spiritual Dis-Integration

Christ is the foundation of the whole educational enterprise in a Catholic school.

Vatican Congregation
for Catholic Education
(1977, article 34)

The retreat experience was sort of a vulnerable place for me, and not in a totally positive way. I usually have a positive connotation to that word, "vulnerable," because when we opened up, we became very close to each other. But that word really has a negative connotation when I think about that retreat.

Allen

Catholic high schools are meant to be places not only of education but also of spiritual formation and growth. Faith must be integrated into the school's functions. Catholic schools are one of the Church's methods of evangelization. Catholic schools are to be Christ-centered (United States Catholic Conference, 1973a; Vatican Congregation for Catholic Education, 1977; Vatican Congregation for the Clergy, 1971; Pope John Paul II, 1979). The Vatican Congregation for Catholic Education described the school as "a privileged place in which, through a living encounter with a cultural inheritance, integral formation occurs" (1977, article 26). Formation has both a "horizontal dimension," seen in interpersonal relationships in the school, and a "vertical dimension," seen in prayer (1977, articles 109-111). Sex education requires an element of spirituality (United States Catholic Conference, 1991). Teachers and catechists also need spiritual formation to perform their roles (Vatican Congregation for the Clergy, 1971).

Formation includes the development of conscience and the teaching of social justice (United States Catholic Conference, 1972, 1973a, 1979, 1981; Vatican Congregation for Catholic Education, 1977, 1988; Saint Pius X, 1905; Vatican Congregation for the Clergy, 1971; Pope John Paul II, 1979). The American bishops addressed this as a need in Catholic education: "The fundamental concept in Catholic social teaching is the dignity of the human person. Human dignity and sacredness, present from the moment of conception, are rooted in the fact that every human being is created directly by God in His image and likeness (cf. Genesis 1:26) and is destined to be with Him forever" (USCC, 1979, article 156). The Vatican Congregation for Catholic Education instructed that in Catholic education, students should be taught that the good or evil done to any human being is as if it were done to Jesus himself (1988, article 80). Catholic schools much teach a preferential option for the poor, which includes the lonely and isolated (Vatican Congregation for Catholic Education, 1988, articles 87-91).

How is this integration of spirituality experienced by gay and lesbian students in Catholic high schools? Is their spirituality an integrated part of their lives? These three stories demonstrate an area very little studied concerning gay and lesbian youth: spiritual development. In these stories, it is clear that gay and lesbian students in Catholic high schools experience spiritual dis-integration.

EMILY

Emily graduated in 1991 from a coeducational, diocesan Catholic high school. She attended the school for all four years. The school was in a town of about 60,000 where Emily lived, but the school had only 220 students. The town also had a military post, and some students were the children of military personnel. The military presence in the town added to its conservatism.

Emily is one of only a small number of women who I interviewed who had been sexually active with girls during high school; a much greater percentage of men who I interviewed had been sexually active with other boys in high school. Emily is also very unique in her description of her relationship with Nora, using the term "girlfriend." No other person who I interviewed described their same-sex sexual partner in high school as being a boyfriend or a girlfriend.

Emily's relationship with Nora began when Emily was a freshman and Nora was a sophomore. They were together for seven years and broke up when they were in college. At the time of this interview, Nora was engaged to be married to a man. Emily and Nora were sexually active with each other from the beginning of their relationship. Emily was only thirteen at the time. "I was very young," she acknowledged. "I was in love. But we didn't think that there was any other people in the whole world. In fact, we were going to grow up, get married, and have kids, but we were going to live next door to each other and go on vacations so we could be alone. I wouldn't have come out if it weren't for Nora. She brought it up, initiated everything, and then I was hooked!" Emily and Nora double-dated with two boys who were a couple of years younger than they were. They liked dating younger guys because they did not put as much pressure on them to be sexual. They never went further than kissing with these boys, and they only kissed a few times. Emily felt that she and Nora needed to date "for a cover."

Emily had no perceptions of what gay people were like when her relationship began with Nora. By her junior year, she began to be more informed. Her parents became friends with a lesbian couple, both of whom were former nuns. Also, Emily's mother's brother came out to the family. She also began forming some impressions from students when they began calling certain teachers "queer" and "fag," based on the mannerisms of the teacher or if the teacher was not married or had no children. "First of all, I didn't know there were so many gay people. I don't think I thought of them as any different in any way, except I felt sad because I thought it was something that you always have to hide; nobody ever really knows who you really are, and you can't have children. To me, that was very sad." In her senior year, Emily heard that a city three hours away from her town had gay bars. She and Nora were surprised to hear that such places existed. "We were ready to travel three hours just to see these people to see what they looked like!"

Emily showed me pictures from her high school yearbook as I interviewed her. She showed me a picture of the girls from the homecoming court. They all looked fairly identical, with similar hair styles and dresses. I did not realize at first that Emily was one of them. "I always feel, when I look at that picture, like, 'There's the four sweet girls and a lesbian.' I know it really doesn't, but I just feel like I stand out really big in that picture. I always felt that if my friends knew, they wouldn't be my friends kind of thing. I just think that by looking at that picture, I look like I'm gay. I don't know if they suspected, because I tried so hard to hide it. I just felt like if they knew, they wouldn't be my friends anymore, or they would think so differently of me. Compared to the rest of them, they look so feminine. And I don't see myself as feminine at all, which is funny because others perceive me as very feminine. I wish that I could have been more up-front with people. I always felt like I had on this mask. Nobody really knew who I was." In addition to hiding her sexuality, Emily was also hiding the fact that her father was an alcoholic and that she had been molested by a man in her town when she was a small child.

Emily did have some very homophobic encounters with adults at the school. Interestingly, all of them involved adults who Emily viewed as being gay and who all were religious persons. The first involved her parish priest who was also the chaplain of the high school. Emily had heard that he hired four senior boys to install a hot tub for him at his rectory and that he insisted that the boys take off their shirts while they do this. He then insisted that they join him in the hot tub when they finished the installation. When Emily told her mother about this, her mother shared with her that Emily's uncle (who was gay) had seen the priest in a gay bar (in the town three hours away). Emily really had strong negative opinions of the priest. "I hate him! I can't stand him! I see him, and I get so mad. Because I came out, I said something in Confession, and he told me that I would go to Hell. And I was in the thing where he couldn't see who I was, and he peeked out and looked at me. And he always looked at me like I was not good enough, like I was a bad person. I stopped going to Church— I stopped going to *his* Church. He just angers me to no end!"

Another example was a religion teacher, Mr. Smith, who some of the students started calling "queer." "I specifically remember my religion teacher saying in class, 'Homosexuality is against the Church.

People are born with this sickness, and they can't help it. It's not against God's will unless they act on it.' That's what he said. And I thought, 'I'm going to Hell! I'm going to Hell!' I remember running to my locker and crying, and Nora said, 'What's wrong!?' And I said, 'We're going to Hell!' And Nora said, 'Shut up! Don't talk about that *here.* '" This was the only time Emily ever heard homosexuality mentioned in a classroom setting. "It really turned me against the Catholic religion, because I felt like what he said was true. Not that I was going to go to Hell, but all these people—all these people sitting in this church disapproved of what I was doing. I would go into Church and be totally preoccupied. I'd be like, 'If they knew. . . .'" Emily and Nora would spend the night together on Saturday night and then go to Mass together on Sunday morning and feel guilty. "I didn't like the fact that I felt like nobody *really* knew who I was."

Emily also felt the principal, a nun, was a lesbian. Her parents' lesbian friends had told her that many nuns were lesbians. She suspected her principal because she wore a tie. She also thought her principal was homophobic. "Yeah, it seems kind of backward."

Emily saw the Catholic Church as sexist. She later converted to the Church of Unity. She saw her high school as sexist because the administration did not allow a girl to walk across the stage at graduation because she was pregnant; they did allow the student who fathered the child to walk across, however. She viewed the gay priest as sexist. "He thought he could do whatever he wanted because he was a man and he was a priest." She was concerned about what advice she could give to the Church on the issue of gay and lesbian students in Catholic high schools. "I don't think there's anything you can tell them that they haven't heard. It's a matter of listening, accepting, realizing that it doesn't go away. It isn't something that you can feel and not act on. Like anything else, if you're not true to yourself, you're only hurting more people. Getting married to try to cover it up only hurts a whole family."

Emily broke up with Nora while they were in college. After the break-up, Emily became very depressed and attempted suicide. She then came out to her parents, who accepted her. "I wish I had gotten into therapy earlier. Gay teens need to go to therapy, even if they don't think they need it. It isn't until later that you realize you need it because you feel so different and so outcast and like you don't belong."

BOB

Bob graduated in 1987 from a coeducational suburban Catholic high school run by the local diocese. The school had more than 600 students. Bob attended the school all four years. He stated that the student population came from affluent families; some students received cars as presents for their sixteenth birthdays. This contributed to the atmosphere of the school. "There was always this idea that because we went there, the faculty and the students somehow thought that we were better than other people. We were expected to be just a little bit above others."

Bob was small in high school and a "late bloomer." He was quiet and shy. A small group of students used to make fun of him but not because they thought he was gay. He didn't have his own clique in high school, but he did have friends. He hung around a great deal with friends of his sister, who were just a few years older than he was.

He was very studious, and wanted a career in biology or medicine in the future. He was angry when the school would shorten classes for all-school Masses. He begged his parents to send him to the local public school, which had better science facilities. "I would rather have had a better lab than a new chapel." He did enjoy events at school such as homecoming and other functions that brought students together and were fun. He didn't like sporting events, and quit the band so that he wouldn't have to go to them. "If I didn't like something, I quit." He became more involved with his classmates in his later years in high school. Bob put a great deal of his energy in high school and college into getting good grades. He viewed this as one way to avoid dealing with his homosexuality.

Bob was not very aware of his sexual orientation while he was in high school. He didn't begin to recognize those feelings in himself until he was in college. He came out to himself and his friends when he was twenty-two. He didn't come out to his parents until he was twenty-five, just a few months before these interviews. "When I did come out to myself, it wasn't this long tortuous thing which I think my parents are thinking it was. I just never really thought about it that much in high school." Bob did not date in high school. His parents were proud of him for asking a girl to homecoming his senior year.

She already had a date, but Bob attended as a photographer for the yearbook.

More common than the term "fag" as an insult in his high school were jokes about AIDS, according to Bob. His primary stereotype of gay people was that they were highly promiscuous. This was based on the media coverage of the AIDS epidemic. "It wasn't so much like, 'They're all interior designers.' It was more like a personification of sexuality." One faculty member was thought by students to be gay because he was not married, even though he was only in his twenties. The only time homosexuality was ever discussed in class was when a girl gave a presentation on homosexuality for a religion class, which was well received.

Bob liked very much a group of students known as peer listeners. "It was pretty much the only positive thing I felt the campus ministry ever did. The people in it were all very easy to talk to and good listeners, and never did judge at all." He did, however, know of a couple cases where the peer listener did share some information with the campus ministry staff about some things students had told them. The campus ministers called these students to their offices and threatened to call their parents; they were upset that the teens were not acting as proper students from *this* high school.

"The people who ran the campus ministry I did not feel were that caring most of the time." One priest who was a campus minister also taught Bob's religion class during his junior year. In class, he was required to select a newspaper article each week on a social topic and write a commentary on it. Bob wrote on subjects such as abortion, homosexuality, interracial marriage, etc. All his papers were returned to him because they "did not conform to Catholic teaching." He remembered this very clearly. "It's weird how things like that stick with you." He failed the class because he refused to rewrite the papers. "I guess I didn't like being told what to think. Everything in high school was presented in black-and-white, but it's a world of grays. They need to remember that theology exists because of *discussion*." Bob's mother had been a Baptist, and she knew the Bible very well. She would help him with his assignments. "In my view, the Catholic Church has all been based on Jesus and the New Testament. All that mumbo-jumbo stuff in the Old Testament, I just threw that out. Unless Jesus said something specifically about it, then you couldn't really say for sure. So on the homosexuality one, I asked my mom for help. We both looked in the Bible, and she said, 'Well, I guess it's *Love everybody,* because that's what He said.' And that's what I put in there, just basically that and 'casting the first stone' and that kind of stuff. And evidently I was *wrong.* I was really wrong, according to the priest."

His parents respected his decision to stop going to Mass when he was in college. He has recently begun going back to Mass at Dignity, a gay Catholic organization. He felt strongly that the Church needed to recognize same-sex unions and was encouraged that the Church was at least discussing the topic more in recent years. He also believed that education about homosexuality needed to take place in the broader context of education about cultural diversity, which he also believed was lacking in Catholic schools.

Some of the pressure of avoiding his sexual orientation resulted in substance abuse for Bob. "I was diagnosed with attention deficit disorder, so they had me on Dexedrine at that time. Well, Dexedrine is speed, and anything I did interacted with it, it seemed. There was no problem getting stuff in school, and by senior year I was running around a lot with friends of my sister who were in college, and they drank a lot. So, that was how I dealt with it, drugs and alcohol. I guess I was very lonely, not having a lot of friends and stuff. Although it's not fun to think about high school, it's always there. It affected me later in life. It really did. For two months I was in rehab." Bob used drugs and alcohol directly to avoid homosexual feelings. "I'd be at a party with my sister's friends, and I'd see somebody, and it'd be like, 'Wow! They're cute!' or something like that. And I'd do that, and I'd be like, 'You need a vodka! You need something straight up!' I guess it was just easier to get sloshed and not really have any recollection of what happened than to sit and ponder and think about it."

In college, Bob went into a rehab center. He quit all drugs including Dexedrine. It was at that time that he came out to himself, his sister, and his friends. His sister had already suspected that he was gay. "She sort of knew there was something more to it. She didn't want to ask me in case it wasn't true. She didn't want to embarrass me or embarrass herself." He decided not to come out to his parents at that time; he also did not tell them about being in rehab. "It was my sense that it's my life, and these are my problems, and I have to deal with them. No one else should have to deal with them. Mom and Dad should not have to be brought into this." He worried that the stress of coming out about his sexuality and his drug problems would be too much for his parents. "I was really worried it could tear the family apart." When he did come out to his parents, his mother told him that she had already reached that conclusion years before.

His parents were very supportive of him once he came out to them, which was important to Bob. "Their love really is unconditional for me, and that meant a lot to me." They discussed why it had taken him so long to come out to them. "Mom said, 'Oh, you worried we would kick you out. We'd never do that.' And I was like, 'I didn't know *what* you'd do. I have friends who were kicked out of the house. You can say this *now,* now that I'm twenty-five. But what if I were sixteen or seventeen and I came out to you in high school or college and you knew I'd still be living at home for five or six years? What were you going to do, quiz me where I went every weekend?'" He gave his parents some books to read to help them adjust. The fact that his father hugged him the next time they met meant a great deal to Bob. "That was more physical than he had been with me for years! I knew everything was going to be all right."

ALLEN

Allen attended all four years at an urban, all-boys high school run by a men's order. He graduated in 1987. There were about 900 students. Although Allen was very religious in high school, he still experienced dis-integration with his spirituality.

Allen felt particularly safe with a number of teachers; he used words such as "nurturing" to describe many of them, in particular, his music teacher. He described the choir as "a second family" and the director as "someone who would never do anything to hurt anyone. He was kind of a parental figure." He made many of his close friendships in the choir. Another place Allen felt safe was the yearbook room. He was the editor of the yearbook in his senior year, and he described the room as "like home." He enjoyed being a photographer for the yearbook partly because it allowed him to connect with other groups of students with whom he would not have been involved, such as the baseball team. "Even though I wasn't on the team, I was part of the group." He traveled with the team to their games to take photos.

One sports group that made him uncomfortable was the football team. He associated them with violence, but could not articulate why. Allen also said that many of the students who played football came from very affluent families. He was uncomfortable at a party he attended given by one of these students. "It was sort of like, 'Yeah, this guy's invited me to his home, but I'm not really in his world.'" Also, many of the football players were Irish. Allen's parents were Italian immigrants, and he lived in a working-class home. He also admitted he was uncomfortable around black and Hispanic kids in his school. Allen said, in high school, he would have never admitted to himself that he had negative feelings about anyone. He always tried to be nice and focus on the positive aspects of people.

Allen felt uncomfortable in situations with girls. When the choir would perform at a girls' school, his friends would be very excited, but Allen just felt uncomfortable. One friend challenged Allen a great deal because he put pressure on him to date. Allen's parents also put pressure on him to date and bring a girl home for them to meet.

Allen was not very comfortable with his home life. He liked school activities because they gave him an excuse to stay away from his home. Allen had been molested by an uncle when he was a small child.

One priest who taught in the school made Allen feel uncomfortable because he was very effeminate and also not a nice person. "He liked the ballet and things like that. He was also very judgmental and condescending. He actually said some nasty things about Italians in class. The school had traditionally been an Irish school. I didn't like him, and I saw him as 'queeny,' which also made me uncomfortable because I didn't think I should be having those thoughts about a priest. I thought that was a bad thing to think about anybody."

Allen was very religious, and during high school he considered entering the priesthood in the future. "When I was in high school, my religious experiences—my experiences of going to Mass—were sort of transcendent and also consoling. It sort of took me out of myself and helped me to think about a world where everything would work out in the end, even if it was difficult. I had this whole martyr struggle thing and it related to my feelings about fitting in and having trouble fitting in. I used to watch the whole group of priests when they would concelebrate Mass together, and it seemed like there was this power there, and I wanted to someday have this power. Sort of facing the world and not being afraid of anything."

Allen was very involved in campus ministry and helped out on the retreats in his high school. The retreats posed a challenge for him. "The retreats were very positive experiences for me, but there was still something I felt was unsafe about them. On one retreat I was helping to give, I got into this long conversation with one of the guys, and I sort of started to come out to him and also tell him about being molested. What happened, basically, was that I started addressing my own issues in the retreat, which was not appropriate to my role; we were supposed to be there for the other people. I also knew that I really wanted to get into it. I sort of got into trouble with the campus minister for that. The retreat experience was sort of a vulnerable place for me, and not in a totally positive way. I usually have a positive connotation to that word, 'vulnerable,' because when we opened up, we became very close to each other. But that word really has a negative connotation when I think about that retreat."

Allen had a conversation with the campus minister, a priest, about the possibility of a religious vocation and about his struggle with his sexual identity. The priest made an interesting comment. "He said, 'You know, a lot of people say that there are a lot of gay priests, but I've never met any at all.'" Allen did appreciate that this priest also shared some information with him from the Kinsey report. "He said that whatever I decided, he would still love me, because he looks at the person." Allen considered this a very positive experience for him.

Allen recognized that he was attracted to some of his friends in high school. His best friend, Dennis, was the first person to whom he confided about being molested and about the possibility that he was gay. He described his feelings toward him as "a schoolgirl crush." They spent hours with each other after school and also talking on the phone together. He also realized that he had very strong sexual feelings toward some other friends. One friend, Bill, made Allen very uncomfortable. "He unnerved me. He was really sort of dangerous to me because I was so attracted to him. I'm surprised I remember this so clearly, because I have no idea of what I did with those feelings. I'm surprised I would even conceive of them in so clear a way." None of Allen's friends or peers thought of him as gay when he was in high school.

Allen said that he mostly ignored or hid his sexual feelings while he was in high school. He also believed he was confused at this time. "I really connected that fact that I had been abused to my sexual feelings. I really put those two together. That was very vexing to me, very distressing. I did talk about it with my campus minister and one or two friends. I interpreted a lot of my feelings in ways that—like it was *not* a gay paradigm. It was another paradigm. It was not about sexual orientation. I figured I didn't like girls and didn't feel comfortable around them because I had been abused when I was small. And possibly I liked guys because I was around guys all the time and because I was abused. I also thought that I had confused two things. I had confused my friendship with these guys for physical attraction. I decided, 'What is happening here is that I've confused physical feelings for friendship; I've conflated these two things for some reason. And my business for the future for myself is to, like, disentangle these two things. I've put these two things together, and I'm going to take them apart. Physical attraction should not be toward my friends.' That was my understanding of what had happened. And I thought about this a lot because it was a big part of my life. *It kept coming up!* Whether it was my parents wanting me to date a girl, or a dance at school, or talking about sex with my friends, it kept coming up!"

REFLECTIONS

I could find no resources from other researchers to help in the reflections for this chapter. It appears that the spiritual development of gay and lesbian youth is an almost-untouched subject. I will relate some data from my survey studies, however. Five items on the surveys dealt with the Church's responsibilities to gay and lesbian people. It is interesting to note that in every comparison and with both the 1990 and 1995 surveys, agreement with these statements was always lower than agreement with statements about the rights of gay and lesbian people. It would appear that not only are gay and lesbian youth spiritually dis-integrated, but so too are their peers on this topic; even for those who believe that gay and lesbian people have rights, they tend to see the Church as having very little responsibility in preserving those rights or serving this population pastorally. The low numbers in both studies are disturbing, especially of males, who agreed with the item, "All people (gay, lesbian, and heterosexual) are children of God." I did find some hope in the 1990 study, however. The greater the length of time males spent in Catholic education, the more likely they were to agree that the Church has responsibilities to gay and lesbian people.

The stories in this chapter point to a problem experienced by some gay and lesbian students in Catholic high schools. Although most of the people I interviewed never heard any negative comments coming from faculty or staff in their high schools, those who did usually heard them in a religious context. This was true also for Mark and Sue (Chapter 3), and for Patty (Chapter 4). One of the counselors who I interviewed, Ms. Krew, had experienced this in her own school. She had been a counselor for two years at her urban-residential all-girls high school run by a women's order. She had worked as a counselor and teacher at another all-girls Catholic high school for four years before this. A religion teacher at her school showed an antigay film put out by the religious right called *The Gay Agenda*. When Ms. Krew went to the principal to complain about this, the principal sided with the teacher.

Another difficulty that gay and lesbian students face in Catholic high schools is a reliance on sharing, especially at retreats, for spiritual growth. I don't mean at all to criticize this practice as a whole. As a campus minister and former parish director of religious education, I know the importance of sharing to help youth grow spiritually. All of us who work with youth, however, need to realize that for gay and lesbian youth, this can be a very threatening activity, as in the story of Allen. Several other persons whom I interviewed also felt uncomfortable on retreats in high school for this very reason.

Although many students in Catholic high schools feel uncomfortable if they perceive religion to be forced upon them, I was surprised how strongly this impacted the people I interviewed. This seemed to be an especially strong feeling for lesbians such as Sue (Chapter 3) and Patty (Chapter 4).

Emily's story points to another religious difficulty experienced by some of the people I interviewed. Often the faculty and staff members who the students perceived as the most homophobic were also perceived as being gay themselves; often they were priests, nuns, brothers, or religion teachers. Larry's story, in Chapter 3, of being harassed in front of a class by a nun whom he also thought was a lesbian is important to remember here. Dan's story of a priest in Chapter 6 is a very disturbing account of this phenomenon. Two of the counselors I interviewed, Mr. Alberts and Brother Peter, experienced this in their schools.

The experiences in Catholic high schools of many of the people who I interviewed left them not just out of the Catholic Church but also very angry with it. This can be seen in Emily's story in this chapter, as well as with Becky (Chapter 2), Mark (Chapter 3), Kevin (Chapter 4), Alice (Chapter 4), and many others.

How well have Catholic high schools contributed to the integration of spirituality into the lives of gay and lesbian students? As I pointed out in the previous chapter, religion was a comfort for some of the people I interviewed. Most often this comfort came as an escape, however. The stories in this chapter show that religion was anything but a comfort for some. It contributed to their turmoil. Their experience did not leave them with an "integration of faith with life"; in fact, it left them spiritually dis-integrated, and sometimes seeking healing outside the Catholic Church.

Chapter 6

Identity Dis-Integration

Sexuality *refers to a fundamental component of personality in and through which we, as male or female, experience our relatedness to self, others, the world, and even God.*

United States Catholic Conference (1991, p. 9)

I don't think that I ever really thought that being a lesbian was really an option. It just wasn't. I grew up in a home where there was a man and woman and these three boys, and they went out with girls, and I was supposed to go out with a boy. I never knew a lesbian. I just didn't think about it. It just wasn't an option.

Denise

The theme of integration, so central to the Catholic philosophy of education, is very clear when the Church's magisterium has spoken about sexuality; sexuality must be seen as integrated with the whole person as an element of his or her identity.

Catholic sex education recognizes sexuality as an intrinsic part to the whole of the student's person (United States Catholic Conference, 1979, 1981). The Church, in being called to educate the whole person, must provide sex education. Sexuality is tied to a person's uniqueness. It exists within the unity of the body and soul. All human beings are sexual beings from the moment of their conceptions. Jesus was a sexual being because he was fully human (United States Catholic Conference, 1981). "Education in human sexuality focuses on development of the total Christian person, along with the development of the family and community" (United States Catholic Conference, 1981, p. 67). "Sexuality refers to a fundamental component of personality in and through which we, as male or female, experience our relatedness to self, others, the world, and even God" (United States Catholic Conference, 1991, p. 9).

This view is echoed by the Vatican Congregation for Catholic Education (1983). Sexuality is recognized as a fundamental component of personality. It is an integral part of the development of personality and the educational process and characterizes a person physically, psychologically, and spiritually. "Affective sex education" considers the person in totality: biologically, psychologically, affectively, socially, and spiritually. It educates the whole person—the intellect, the will, feelings, and emotions.

Catholic philosophy of education is tied to Catholic philosophy of sexuality; sexuality is an integrated part of identity. It is in the identity development of the student that family, school, social relations, faith, curriculum, and sexuality should come together and be integrated. How is sexuality integrated into identity for gay and lesbian students in Catholic schools? The following three stories demonstrate one of the most important themes in my study: gay and lesbian youth in Catholic education experience identity dis-integration.

NICK

Nick grew up in a town with a population of 10,000 to 15,000 people. He attended the area's Catholic high school for four years and graduated in 1993. His high school had about 800 students, was coeducational, and was run by the local diocese. Nick had recently come out to himself and a few other people around him when I interviewed him. His journey to self-acceptance has been difficult.

Nick had a long history of trouble in his family before he began high school. He came from an affluent family; he described them as "distant, not very affectionate." He had been in therapy since he was a small child for problems with his father and for having attention deficit disorder. Poor grades greatly influenced family tensions. During his high school years, his father beat him with a belt on a number of occasions, and his mother would also strike him. Nick was often punished for small infractions. If he chewed with his mouth open at dinner he was forced to eat in the basement, or if his clothes were not folded properly they were thrown on the floor. "Everything had to be perfect." He did enjoy spending time at his grandmother's house, which was nearby.

When he entered high school, his peers began to tease him. Some teasing was about being gay, but most of it concerned his size; Nick was small for his age. "Maybe someone would say, 'Look how he walks!' or something like that. They called me 'fag, faggot, queer, fucking queer.' I felt very put down. I got very defensive. I'd either shut up and feel bad or try to poke fun back. I had really low self-esteem. Externally, I'd try to act macho. I'd try to go along with what everyone else was saying, talk about girls, and just try to ignore what was said." At the time he was in high school, he knew of no other student who received this kind of treatment.

Nick hated math class; he was deficient in the subject and felt that his teacher didn't care about his performance and he was also frightened by some violence he experienced there. "There was this one guy in the class that, I don't know why—walking out of class one day, he just nailed me. I don't know why; he just hit me. Also, walking the hallways one year, I was getting bullied. I remember I literally had to reroute my walk to class to avoid this guy. I hated walking through the hallways, and I used to get nauseated doing it." In the cafeteria, Nick would eat by himself or sometimes with just one or two friends. He had to spend time in the lunchroom before school began each day, and he would become nervous thinking about what would happen.

Nick performed poorly in academic subjects. He felt demeaned when he was required to visit the guidance office for academic counseling, as all students did. He felt that he couldn't discuss himself, his home, or his social life at school with his guidance counselor. He also didn't feel very supported by some of his teachers. "One time I was in class and there was this guy who was picking on me. And I got up and picked up a religion book and just smacked him in the back of the head with it 'cause I was sick and tired of all the shit. After class, the teacher talked to me and said, 'What if you had had a brick?' It was just total bullshit. No one seemed to ask any questions, or asked 'Why?' or wanted to see where I was coming from." Nick wished that his school had had a more diverse faculty, including some gay and lesbian teachers who could have been role models.

He found some aspects of religion comforting. "I just really liked going to church, probably because it was out of the home and I could just sit there and be relaxed and calm and at peace and not have to worry about this and that, just for that short period of time. But I knew when we left that everything would start up again. It was just one of the few places I could go and just take a sigh and be like, 'Okay, I don't have to deal with this right now.'"

Nick had no recollection of any significant things being said in his high school about the Church's opposition to homosexuality. Possibly a few things were mentioned when discussing Sodom and Gomorrah in Scripture class. He was surprised, when he attended a Catholic university, to discover that the Church was opposed to homosexuality. "You know, raised with the whole loving, caring, every-one-is-equal sort of attitude, and then you hear conversations lately; 'The Catholic Church doesn't condone this' and 'Their view is that homosexuality is wrong.' And just sort of a whole negative attitude, it's really surprised me." He did see the Catholic identity of his high school as possibly contributing to silence on the topic in the curriculum.

Because he was not accepted socially, activities became very important for Nick. "I didn't have very many friends in high school, and we didn't seem to *do* much together. So it was important for me to *do* stuff together with people in high school." He enjoyed playing in the band, going to basketball games, belonging to the Boy Scouts and to a martial arts group, being in art class, working after school, and any activities where he felt "included and accepted." He often found adult role models and friends in these activities.

The locker rooms and bathrooms were uncomfortable places for Nick. "Locker rooms in gym class I just hated because there was just this one place I could go and I wouldn't be messed with or picked on or anything like that. It was this bench. Everybody else always used lockers, but I never did. It was just this one place I could get out of the locker room quick and easy. Bathrooms were another place where I just felt nervous and tense. It was like a closed place where if I was ever getting messed with or picked on, I really couldn't do anything about it." There were many gay jokes told in the locker rooms, but generally not directed specifically at Nick. Some of his discomfort had to do with the nudity involved in these situations. "You're a freshman, and you're fifteen years old, and you know that if you get a hard-on in the shower you're going to get ridiculed and all kinds of stuff like that. I was very careful at times, you know. I was very careful about fantasies and experiences and whatever. Just my whole atmosphere with life, with family, and everything, I was just very closed about it all."

Nick's sexual experiences began with boys just before his freshman year in high school. One boy was a neighbor; they had sex with each other a few times, but never discussed it after that. Another boy was in Boy Scouts with Nick and they also had sex a few times together.

Nick dated a few girls in high school, and he had sex with one girlfriend a few times. "I really didn't know if I was good-looking, so I really didn't know if I could have a girlfriend."

Nick had very vague impressions of gay people, and none of them were positive. Nick recognized as gay the Boy Scout with whom he had had sex. "His mannerisms were effeminate. No one liked him, and people made fun of him." He also recognized a store clerk in town as gay because he too had effeminate mannerisms. "I could identify him just from what my friends would say about gays. He just didn't act like everyone else." This added to Nick's confusion. "I was like, 'Well, that's not how I am, so how could I be gay?'" He also had even more negative impressions of gay people. "Dirty old men, sort of shady characters, out looking for young boys or something. Very deviant, lurking in the shadows." This was also an image with which he could not identify.

His school provided no help in clarifying a gay identity for him. Homosexuality was never discussed there. Nick did find a very small amount of information in some books in the library. His family also did not give any help. Other than his father asking him if he was gay, the topic was never discussed in his home. "I came from a very conservative Roman Catholic family, and a homosexual's life was just not the life of the family. It was not part of our everyday life."

The road to self-identifying was very unclear for Nick. "At fifteen, my dad asked me if I was gay, and that sort of struck me. I'd had different gay fantasies around that time, and a couple of encounters. I just thought that was part of life or whatever that every kid went through. But I also thought personally that I was having one or two more than everyone else was having. I mean, I wasn't open about any of that stuff at fifteen. I was very closed. I didn't talk much. It was hard sometimes as the years went on because at different times it would come up, and at certain times it was more latent than others. So, whenever it came up, I just dealt with it by myself, personally, individually. And that was the end of it for that time 'til the next sort of onset, like if I had more gay fantasies." The pressure of these issues became greater for Nick as high school progressed. He began talking to a few other people about it, mostly the mothers of friends he had made through his job. "It was very confusing to me, because by the time that eleventh and twelfth grade came around, I started, 'Am I gay? Am I straight?' I went through this whole thing one year where I talked with friends and their mothers about it. They were like, 'You know, you're going to have to find out.' And I was dead-on, 'I'm *not* gay. *No!* I'm *not!*' I denied it. I was stuck on that. That was what I would say, but in the back of my mind, I would be like, 'Well, are you sure?' In the back of my head, there was always this doubt, like something saying, 'Well, you possibly could be,' or 'You might be,' or 'You are.' I tried to ignore it."

In his freshman year at college, Nick attempted suicide. He said that this was not really related to his homosexuality; the university was just too overwhelming for him.

DAN

Dan attended a high school boarding seminary during his junior and senior years. The school was run by a men's religious order. Although it was a seminary, the focus was less on priesthood preparation and more on student development, according to Dan. A few students did live at home, but most chose to board on campus by their junior year. It was a small school with only fifty students. The class sizes varied greatly as large numbers of students dropped out after freshman and sophomore years. Most students went home on the weekends. The school was located in a suburban area, but its large acreage provided a rural atmosphere.

Dan's family did not want him to attend the seminary. The school had been brought to his attention by a local priest in the town where Dan grew up. The priest was concerned for Dan's welfare because his stepfather was physically abusive. His natural father had abandoned the family. Dan lived with his alcoholic grandfather in junior high, who really didn't take care of him. Dan had to enroll himself in his first two years of public high school. He hated staying with his mother and stepfather over the summers and would try to spend as much time as possible at friends' homes for the duration. The religious order that ran the school allowed Dan to attend free of tuition and provided him with allowances that covered personal expenses. Dan's family never attended the Christmas parties on campus, but Dan enjoyed being with the families of other students. He described this as a kind of escapism; he could be part of a loving, caring family for the holidays. His parents never visited him at the school until graduation day. "They really just didn't share my life." Although there was no overt homophobia in his family, "hush-hush" discussions occurred about a gay cousin of his of whom the family seemed somewhat ashamed.

At seminary, Dan found family warmth in different ways. One was through a Mexican nun who was one of the cooks; she reminded him of his grandmother. The two would go for long walks together hand in hand. "This was the year that I was pretty confused, and I was just dealing with a lot of different issues. And she really made me feel lovable. Even though she spoke more Spanish than English, and it was very difficult communicating with her, I think a lot more was said in just being with her. She really made me feel lovable at a time when I didn't love myself."

Dan enjoyed being a part of the soccer team. He admitted that he was a horrible player, and only made it onto the field about three times each season and only when the opposing team was so far behind that his school could not lose. "When they put me in, it was always incredible because everyone would cheer so loud, the other team would wonder who I was."

Dan also loved the chapel at the school. "I remember many nights going in there to pray and falling asleep on the floor. I really felt a higher presence." He also loved his senior retreat where he could share with his classmates. He felt he grew as a person through the time he spent working with abused children at a public housing project in a nearby city. "I really became an empathic person. I really became sensitive to the needs of the poor."

Dating was allowed on weekends, but girls were not allowed on the campus. Dan and another student double-dated occasionally with two girls who lived nearby. The dating wasn't very serious.

Dan considered himself ugly when he was a high school student. He worried about his weight, and spent a great deal of time working out and running to keep his weight down. "I did a lot of compensation for self-esteem that year. I was always trying to improve the way I looked. I think that went along with having the different roles that I played there. I was senior class president. I was on the yearbook staff. I was involved in the musicals. I was in the choir. I was in soccer, and I felt that was kind of the role you had to play. You had to be physically attractive to be in that kind of a position."

The transition from public high school to seminary was difficult for Dan. "I was very calculated in what I did. I always thought about everything before I did it, what I said before I said it, and was very reflective on what other people were saying and doing around me in an attempt, I guess, to make myself belong, to kind of integrate or connect with the people there. As I entered, I wondered, 'How do I fit into this group?' In a way, I was in control of how I was going to portray myself to these people. But I think what ended up happening over time was I had a very difficult time with the masks, or keeping up the identity, and so it started to come through. A lot of that was baggage taken from my home. I tried to be at first a really spiritual or holy person who prayed often. There was a lot of doing things to get people to like me. There was a lot of going out of my way to do things. It seemed I had the popularity of one set of people and the unpopularity of another set of people. I almost became this double-headed person. It was like there was two of me." The theme of dis-integration can clearly be seen in statements like Dan's.

In his junior year, Dan and some other students dressed in drag for the Halloween party. The administration didn't give them any problem with this but other students did call them "fags" and "queers." Ironically, according to Dan, these same students also dressed in drag the next year. "I think for myself it represented a lot of confusion and insecurity. I was really searching for something that made me unique, and I would do a lot of extraordinary things to get that status or that label. But I think the underlying emotions behind that were really confusion and insecurity with whom I was." He saw this identity exploration as having as much to do with being an adolescent as being a *gay* adolescent.

The impression that Dan and his peers had of gays was of effeminate men. This impression also seemed to be held by the staff. "Homosexuality was not a subject that was talked about in that environment. It was very taboo by the students and the staff. The staff by their not saying anything about it and their reinforcement of what a man should be and how masculine you should be. Homosexuality didn't tie into their ideal of what a man is, and that only added more baggage for me. A gay person was effeminate, had female characteristics, like limp wrists, not into sports, not masculine, walked differently than other men, you know." Some students were effeminate and were called "fags" by other students. This never happened to Dan, except at the Halloween party. "I think I worked hard at keeping as masculine an appearance as I could, because I had seen the way they treated other students that acted feminine. It wasn't only a thing with other peers; it was also a formational issue a lot of times. A character issue was that a male student was not supposed to act that way. They really made an effort; if you were feminine, they really tried to 'butch you up,' so to speak. It would be brought up in your evaluation if they thought you were taking on feminine characteristics."

Dan's first sexual experience was with his roommate during his junior year. He said they were very similar in that both had problems with self-esteem. "It was that whole exploration of another person, another individual, of being sexual with someone, even though nothing was ever consummated. I can just remember our two bodies laying next to one another, and I was just shaking so bad. And I remember, there was a sense of compassion that he had because he knew that I was really kind of scared about it. He brought me back to my bed and then went back to his own bed. I look back on that, and I really allowed myself to be vulnerable with him, and yet he respected me enough not to do anything." Dan also felt that there was a part of his roommate that was very secretive. The boy committed suicide after graduation; he gave little reason in his suicide note for his actions.

Dan began having more sexual encounters with his fellow students. In his senior year, he had sexual encounters with eight to ten of the twenty-four students who were in the junior and senior classes at that time. "It was very secretive. It was done in the dark. Lights were off. All of it was masturbation. We never kissed. There was never any oral sex. It was all done pretty much with me giving the satisfaction and not receiving." Encounters would take place when Dan and another student would be talking late at night in a dorm room. When the other student would fall asleep, Dan would begin to masturbate him. He described his approach as "very calculated." The occurrences became more and more frequent, and Dan felt ashamed about them. "That was kind of my time of feeling like I wasn't in control of my sexuality, like it was running away with me."

Often the other student would pretend to be asleep the entire time. If not, it was always stated between the students that they were not gay. The encounters were never discussed between students. At the time, Dan believed they were isolated. "I thought I was the only person doing that." He perceived these other boys as straight males who were letting him masturbate them. The topic was so "taboo" between students that Dan never knew that his best friend in high school was sexually active and involved with another male student. Many years passed before they shared this information.

Although there were jokes and teasing about homosexuality among students, the topic was never seriously discussed. It was also never discussed in classes or in spiritual formation. Dan never discussed it with anyone, not even in Confession. The only touchy subject discussed in spiritual direction was masturbation, but this was never seriously discussed among students. Dan did decide to bring up the topic with the associate pastor in his home parish over a break. This resulted in a sexual encounter with the priest. Dan stated that the priest was not very helpful in talking about the issues with him. "It seemed that everyone was in denial."

It was a common practice in the school for each upperclassman to take on and mentor a lowerclassman. Sometimes, the two would sleep in one bed together on weekends in the dorms. Dan didn't think that these were always sexual relationships, however. The administration did nothing to stop the practice because to do so would have forced them to discuss homosexuality, according to Dan. He also noted that there was a faculty member who was a pedophile living in the dorm, and he probably didn't want to bring attention to the issue.

"We had a pedophilia case at the high school seminary when I was there, and it was very hush-hush, you know. When I was in high school, sexually, I knew what was going on only because it was that age when you're exploring. But I don't think that that says you're capable of maintaining a relationship or that that person, that adult, should involve you in something like that."

Although Dan was more definite about his sexuality than many other persons I interviewed, it cannot be said that he had integrated his sexuality into his identity. "I knew—I think I knew at the time that I was gay, and I didn't want to admit it. I think that's where the secrecy came in, the doing it at night in the dark, you know. It was a dark part of myself that I didn't want other people to know about. It was a horrible, bad, evil part of myself. All the going out of my way to be nice to people, I was probably compensating in a way. I was making up for being gay, but also not wanting to admit it. I thought it would be a better thing if I were heterosexual, but because I wasn't, I would have to work harder at portraying this image of being someone normal. I think I knew I was gay, I'd have to say, when I was in fifth or sixth grade; there was more attraction to boys than to girls."

Dan did have a boyfriend in his senior year. The two actually planned sexual meetings, encounters that were limited to masturbation and rubbing against each other with their clothes on. Dan broke off this relationship when he was a freshman in college because he developed a new relationship there.

At the end of his junior year, Dan began having a very strange relationship with a priest who was the dean of his dorm. The priest at first seemed to dislike Dan intensely. "One time when I was coming back from running, he pulled me into his room and really laid into me about working out so much. I said something like, 'I'm not good at sports, and I really want to keep my shape up.' And he said, 'Why don't you work on getting a personality first!' or something like that. It was at that point that I started to feel alienated, and I really felt that he tried to alienate me from the other members of my class. We elected officers at the end of the year for the coming year. When they elected me senior class president, I heard him in the other room talking with the students. He said, 'Are you sure you want him as your class president? I think you're making a big mistake.' And all my classmates said, 'No, we think he'll do a good job.'"

The priest left the high school after Dan's junior year to work at the house of formation for the order at a Catholic university. When he announced that he was leaving, he told Dan he would miss him. Dan was surprised at this. The two began a correspondence in Dan's senior year. "I sort of transferred my desire for a father who would be proud of me onto him." Dan had decided to enter the order and went for a visit to the house of formation in his senior year. While visiting, he and the priest had some "semisexual" encounters, such as sitting on the priest's lap and wrestling with him. In the summer between high school graduation and his first year in college, Dan and the priest became sexually active. Dan was seventeen at the time, and he was nineteen when the relationship ended.

While he was at the house of formation, the relationship became less personal and more physical. Dan said he "became like a spouse" to the priest. Dan never experienced orgasms when with the priest; the focus was always on the priest's satisfaction. After the experiences, the priest would literally throw him out of his quarters, and would also give some confusing messages to Dan. "Here we would be, me performing oral sex on him, and he would say, 'Well, now, this doesn't make you a homosexual because you do this.'"

Dan had different reactions to the overall seminary experience in high school in different interviews. In one interview, he was looking at a picture of the school on the cover of his yearbook. "When I think of what this means to me, I think of a nurturing environment. At first, it was just a kind of tumultuous time in my life, and then it became a very, very happy time in my life." In another interview, however, he had recently visited some people from the order. This brought back many memories for him. "I found it to be a more nurturing environment than what I had come from, than my home environment. But looking back, I don't think it was a healthy environment. There were certain standards that I was expected to meet, which I don't think are all bad. At the same time, I was always made to feel like I was an average person. When I went to college with the order, the high school told the house superiors not to expect too much from me academically. They weren't interested in focusing on peoples' strengths, but rather focusing on their weaknesses. They sort of took a look at you and boxed you into a category. The whole time I was there, I was really made to think about, 'What are my problems? What's wrong with me? What are the issues I need to work on?' I was always made to feel the shame, the guilt, the hurt, and always thinking, 'I have some formation issue,' and 'I always have something to deal with,' and 'I can't get on with my life until I get through this.' I think that feeling ugly and out of shape and working out all the time had something to do with this. You know, these people were my family for a time, and they really didn't care what I had done with my life. They didn't care about my accomplishments now. You know, I'm much happier now than when I was in the order. I have a better relationship with God. I'm much more of a man of prayer. The values that we talked about, I'm living."

Dan had mixed reactions as an adult to the Church's position on homosexuality. While he acknowledged that the Church's theology was underdeveloped, he also saw Catholic people as more accepting of gay and lesbian people and people with AIDS than most Protestant churches.

DENISE

Denise graduated from high school in 1987. She grew up in a somewhat affluent suburban neighborhood, but she attended an all-girls Catholic high school in an urban residential area. The school was run by a women's religious order. Most of the other 300 students lived near the school and came from working-class families. Denise attended three years at the school; she spent her sophomore year overseas. She had attended public school through junior high, then her parents became concerned with her behavior in school and decided to enroll her in a school with less pressure concerning dating boys. Her mother worked near the Catholic school and could drop her off in the morning and pick her up on the way home.

Denise felt very comfortable at her high school, and preferred it over public school. "Where I went to high school was just generally a safe environment. It was all women. It was very, very forgiving. I don't remember there being a lot of dogma. I'm sure it was present, but I really didn't pay any attention to it. My parents were Catholic, but I had already turned all that off by the time I went to high school. It was just all really safe. I felt like, when I went to a public junior high that was coed, in order to be accepted by boys or to be liked or to hang around with them, I had to be provocative in some way or sexual in some way. I objectified myself to be comfortable with them. And my mother picked up on this and she wanted me to go somewhere where I could concentrate on school. The fact that it was all girls and we had uniforms made looks not really an issue. Plus I had skipped school *a lot* in junior high, and this wasn't so easy in high school."

"I didn't like high school because I had huge self-esteem problems, and I didn't feel like academics were coming that easily for me." Denise's home situation also made things difficult for her. Her father traveled a great deal and her mother also worked. As a result, she had been put in a situation of making adult decisions at an early age. She had made some bad decisions and had recognized this. "I developed this sense that, 'I'm not very good. I'm not very smart. I make not very smart choices. I make bad decisions. I hang around with bad friends.' I felt insecure. I never felt like I looked good or talked well."

Although Denise made friends at her school, she didn't seem to feel very connected to the other girls. She did have a clique of friends. "But I didn't feel any sense of loyalty to them. I don't remember feeling great about being in my little clique. It was just like this group of people who I ate lunch with." While Denise liked her high school, she did feel different from her peers there. "I felt disconnected and out of place. Partly it was because I *was* different from many of those girls. I grew up Catholic, but I didn't believe in the dogma. I didn't believe in God. Even if they didn't believe in God, they wouldn't have said it because it was not accepted, and I was very outspoken; I talked back. I had political opinions. I just didn't fit in. That's how it felt to me. I felt different, and I don't know why that was. I was pro-choice. They were pro-life. I'm sure there were kids in that school who were pro-choice, but they just didn't come out and say it. I would say it in theology class. I felt very different. I felt out of place."

Denise spent little time associating with fellow students outside school. Most after-school time was spent with friends in her neighborhood that she had made in public school. Although she seemed to have closer relationships with these friends in the neighborhood, she also admitted that in addition to being more sophisticated than her classmates, her neighborhood friends were also more judgmental. "In some ways, I felt more comfortable at school because the students there were more working class. I didn't feel that I was going to be judged for not having something or not knowing something or being aware of something."

She did have one experience of peer pressure at her high school that she remembered very clearly from her freshman year. The school had a tradition of older students taking freshmen under their wings. Denise's "big sister" expected her to be a partier and smoke marijuana. They went to a party together, and Denise got very drunk and stoned and became frightened. "At that time, I felt like in order to be accepted I had to do what somebody else did. So if they did it, and I didn't do it, they wouldn't like me." The older girl expressed disappointment that Denise was not especially into drugs and that she had lied about her experience with them.

Religion was not very important to Denise. Her parents were liberal Catholics. They sent her to a Catholic school for behavioral, not religious reasons. They allowed her to stop going to Mass when she chose. "In school, we weren't forced to go to Mass. You could go to Mass or go to study time. I would go to study time unless I was really tired. Then, I would go to Mass and take a nap, because you couldn't nap in study time."

She often argued her positions in class fiercely. "I *had* to be right." Her instructors did not have negative reactions when she spoke up. They just told her that it was her opinion, but that it was also against Church teaching. She got into trouble once for talking back, but she was told that it wasn't what she had said, but rather how she had said it. She did advocate for gay rights in class discussions. "I was such an advocate for gay rights in high school. Oh, I was *so* passionate. But it never occurred to me that I was gay. I just felt very strongly about it." Homosexuality was not discussed in classrooms unless Denise brought it up. She saw herself as "always rooting for the underdog." She also advocated for the small number of black students in her school. Although the school did not discuss the topic, she knew that the Church taught that homosexuality was a sin because of a homily given by the priest in her home parish. She didn't react very strongly to this at the time because she didn't agree with the Church on many things. She was concerned about the Church's teaching as an adult. "They should really say to themselves, 'Are we really creating more harmony in the world, or are we just creating more disbalance?'"

Denise's perceptions of her sexual identity were ambiguous in high school. "I was really aware at that time of being aroused by looking at women or pornography with women. But I always attributed that to that we really eroticize women's bodies, and most women are aroused by looking at women's bodies, like on the cover of *Cosmopolitan*. I really was not aware."

Denise did talk about sexuality with fellow students in school. "I didn't talk about my arousal, but we did talk about pornography. We looked at it together. We talked about the women, like 'Oh wow. She's so beautiful,' whatever you would say. I do remember, though, that I focused more on the men than on the women even though I don't think I really meant it. People would say, 'He's so hot!' And I would like not get it, but I would say, 'Oooo yeah. He's really hot!'"

Denise was sexually active with boys in high school. "I did not enjoy having sex with boys in high school. I did it because I thought it was a way I could get some affection and attention or something. I didn't really enjoy it. It was okay, but it was just kind of there. But I really was not clued into that." She was introduced to pornography by watching it with boys when she was about to have sex with them. "It was just a lot of experimentation and trying to find out who I was. And I'm sure a lot of these boys were just trying to find out who they were. Yeah, it's such a shame that at a time when you are trying to find out who you are, you're looking at these pictures. It's such an objectification. What a way to learn about sexuality. What a way to learn about how to become aroused. I wouldn't want it for my own child."

"I don't think that I ever really thought that being a lesbian was really an option. It just wasn't. I grew up in this home where there was a man and woman and these three boys, and they went out with girls, and I was supposed to go out with a boy. I never knew a lesbian. I just didn't think about it. It just wasn't an option. If it was an option, I probably would have done it. I find it interesting that I can't be more articulate about this." Denise perceived herself as being unfeminine in high school; she talked back, cussed, and didn't worry very much about her appearance. This began when she was much younger. "When I was a little girl, I wanted to be a boy." Her mother encouraged her to act more refined in high school. Denise worried in high school that she would not find a husband later in life.

Denise had very limited perceptions of lesbians in high school. "My mom worked at a hospital, and she had a friend who was a nurse, a man, who was gay. And he used to come over to the house. But that was like a man thing. Men did that. He was kind of a queen." She couldn't remember thinking of any of her classmates as lesbians. Her peers didn't perceive her as gay either, "because I always had a boyfriend and I had long hair." There was some joking about homosexuality with fellow students, but most rumors about girls dealt with sex with boys and pregnancy. She did think that the principal and another nun were in love. She admired the principal a great deal for her boldness, but was also concerned because she was not very attractive. "Maybe that's part of the whole thing about being a lesbian. I didn't look like Sister Loretta, and I didn't want to." She never heard any other students speculate that the principal was a lesbian. Denise also attended women's college, where she saw more lesbians.

"In college, I started to find myself really more attracted to women, but I still didn't really know how I felt or what to do with that or what that would mean. I think I started to get in touch with the losses if I went in that direction. I remember wanting to have a normal, mainstream, middle-class kind of life. So I ended up getting married. And it wasn't until I got married that I was like, 'Oooo, I really don't like this. This really isn't me. I tried it. It's not going to work.' Then I realized that I wanted to go in another direction. But it took a lot. I had to do that whole bride fantasy thing and get that out of my system before I could go on."

She saw the coming-out process as different for women than for men. "When I came out, I heard from people, 'You won't have children. You're going to lose the privilege you get from being connected to a male in this society.' But for men coming out, it's, 'You're going to get bashed. You're going to be in physical danger all the time. You're going to get AIDS.' Not 'You're going to lose some social status,' but 'Your life is going to be really rough.'"

REFLECTIONS

One of the most interesting things I found in my studies was that the people I interviewed had a wide range of awareness of themselves as gay or lesbian when they were in high school. Those who were aware often regarded this aspect of themselves as something to feel bad about or ashamed of. Women who I interviewed tended to simply think that they lacked a sexual drive at all because they were not sexually interested in boys. Most interesting to me was the fact that some, especially men, could have clear homosexual fantasies or even engage in homosexual sex with others and still not think of themselves as gay, such as Nick or Kevin (Chapter 4) or Larry (Chapter 3). Although a number of the people I interviewed had sexual experiences in and before high school with people of the same or opposite sex, this didn't always seem to be helpful for them in discovering their own sexual identities.

The theme of identity dis-integration made sense to most of the counselors I interviewed. Some felt "denial" or "repression" were better words to explain it. Ms. Edwards pointed out that even the Church's teaching on homosexuality was dis-integrated, dividing identity, which is okay, from behavior, which is not okay. One of the counselors, Mr. Alberts, was himself gay, and he strongly agreed with the use of this language to describe the experience. "It's like taking a part of your being and closing it off in scar tissue and setting it aside. But it can never be; you can never feel whole. In fact, you feel like there's a hole in your feelings, thoughts, and being, your spirituality, that can never be addressed. And *that's* dis-integration."

Some of the difficulty in integrating their homosexuality into their identities came from negative stereotypes that the people I interviewed had of gay and lesbian people. These were typically of men who were effeminate and in some way dirty, such as Nick and Dan's descriptions. Very often, there were simply no images of lesbians, as Denise remembered. Recall the words of Patty in Chapter 4 when she described meeting a lesbian woman, "She was just so much like me that I didn't think she was a lesbian. I just thought a lesbian would be somebody totally different, totally beyond my experience. I had no idea what it would look like or anything."

The act of coming out is usually seen as a social act of telling others that one is gay or lesbian, but a step must take place before this—admitting to oneself that one is gay or lesbian. Identity development in gay and lesbian youth has been the subject of much research. Often these youth feel compelled to come out; it is not seen as a free choice for them. They sometimes compartmentalize their homosexuality or fear it, thinking that they will begin to become their negative stereotypes of gay and lesbian people if they come out (Jackson and Sullivan, 1994; Herdt and Boxer, 1993). Some gay and lesbian youth use images of death in describing their experiences of coming to terms with who they are; the identity they had before must die for a new identity to be born. Parental relationships also die metaphorically for these youth (Herdt and Boxer, 1993). They feel a huge pressure to date people of the opposite sex, and some gay and lesbian youth overcompensate by being heterosexually promiscuous (Herdt and Boxer, 1993; DiGiacomo, 1993; Friend, 1993). On the other hand, the isolation these youth experience causes some gay and lesbian adolescents, especially males, to seek out anonymous gay sex rather than experience closeness to no one. Because such experiences are dangerous, some gay males begin to associate their very identities with danger (Rybicki, 1995; Mallon, 1994). They may delay certain adolescent developmental tasks until later because of the energy they must expend in coming out (Durby, 1994). Some may see themselves first as bisexual and then later as homosexual (Mallon, 1994; Herdt and Boxer, 1993). It is clear that the task of identity development has special difficulties for gay and lesbian youth.

Some researchers have described stages of identity development for gay and lesbian youth. These theories began in the 1970s with researchers such as Plummer (1975), Ponse (1978, 1984), and Cass (1979, 1984). I personally prefer the stage model developed by Troiden (1988, 1989). I believe that he offers the most complete picture. A distinction of these models from previous research is that they focus on meaning for the individual. These are not studies of how often a person has sex or thinks about sex, but rather what sexual ideation and sexual behavior mean to the person.

Troiden described four stages of identity development for gay and lesbian youth. He pointed out that these stages are not exact; one could move back and forth through stages, and stages may overlap.

Stage one, *sensitization,* occurs before puberty. The child has a distinct sense of being different. This is not an uncommon experience for all children, but it seems that gay and lesbian children feel more strongly than other children that they are different from their peers and others around them. Savin-Williams (1990) also found this. These youth don't see their differences as having anything to do with sex, but sometimes as not being like other children of the same gender. Although a number of children engage in same-sex sexual exploration, children do not associate sexual activity with sexual orientation.

In stage two, *identity confusion,* the child feels he or she might be homosexual. Now, they feel sexually different from their peers. They are more likely to engage in sexual experiences at this stage and to begin to attribute meaning to them.

In stage three, *identity assumption,* the adolescent begins to tolerate his or her own homosexuality and begins to seek out other gay and lesbian people. By the fourth and final stage, *commitment,* the individual sees homosexuality as an asset and as part of his or her entire identity.

Denise perceived coming out to be different for women than for men. Troiden acknowledges some differences in identity development for men and women. In our culture, men are taught to be sexually active much more so than women. As a result, gay men are likely to be more sexually active in their identity development journey than lesbian women. de Monteflores and Schultz (1978) also found a number of differences between gay men and lesbian women in their coming-out process. Males are more likely to have had homosexual experiences before understanding homosexuality as a concept. If they avoid labeling themselves as "homosexual," adolescent lesbians are more likely to emphasize emotions ("I just really like her as a friend"), while adolescent gay males are more likely to deemphasize emotions ("It's not like I'm in love with him or something"). Calling oneself "homosexual" is more threatening for males than for females.

Jennes (1992) has argued that stage theories do not adequately explain the experiences of lesbians in developing their identities. Her own model, *detypification,* involves the evolving meaning of the concept "lesbian" for the individual. At first, adolescent girls have a socially constructed concept of "lesbian" to which they cannot relate. They do not put themselves into this category. As they slowly gain more valid information about lesbians, this concept changes for each of them. For some, they can begin to put themselves into this category as they begin to understand it differently; they recognize themselves as lesbians. It is impossible in this model for a woman to identify herself as a lesbian without knowing other lesbians.

These theories point to the enormous task faced by gay and lesbian adolescents in doing what every adolescent must do: form an identity. The difficulty is that gay and lesbian adolescents must form an identity that is socially unacceptable, yet they are pushed toward it from within, which is often very confusing for them. Consider the story of Gina in Chapter 2. Her mother was upset because Gina had told her that she had been thinking about being a lesbian for many years, yet the experience was something very new for her.

One area that Dan brings up (and that was also discussed by Patrick in Chapter 2) is the presence of a great deal of sexual activity in high school boarding seminaries. This is certainly a touchy subject, and I intend to tread very carefully around it. It is no great secret that many people believe that a very high number of Catholic clergy are gay. Brother Peter, one of the counselors I interviewed, expressed disgust with the Church's magisterium at continuing to condemn homosexual activity when he believed that so many priests and bishops were gay. Media coverage of many homosexual pedophilia cases in the Church has affected how male religious figures interact with students, and would be a hindrance to discussion of homosexuality in Catholic schools, according to Brother Peter as well as two other counselors, Brother George and Mr. Alberts. Brother Peter also stated that, for many years, he had coached wrestling. While the best way to teach wrestling is to get down on the mat with a student and demonstrate it, he admitted that he had stopped doing this and had started asking older students to teach younger ones because of the fear that has developed over pedophilia in the Church. Clearly, the issue has an impact in a broad range of Catholic education.

Looking more specifically at high school boarding seminaries, I sought some insight from one person in my study of counselors. I interviewed Father Morgan. Although he was not a licensed counselor, he was a spiritual director at a boarding high school seminary and had worked at the school for fourteen years. At first in the interview, Father Morgan was reluctant to admit that this was a common experience. "If you asked a random sample of guys who had attended high school seminary rather than just gay alumni, I don't think that they would have said that sex between students was very common." As the interview progressed, I pointed out that some researchers had found this to be common in other male boarding schools, not just seminaries (Bullough and Bullough, 1978). Later in the interview, he told me, "Well, see, I went to high school seminary, and I had an experience while I was in high school, and I don't see myself as particularly out of the range of normalcy, I guess. So, it doesn't surprise me."

Another interesting discovery was that the people I interviewed had virtually no awareness of the adult gay world when they were in high school. One interviewee lived in the San Francisco Bay area in high school when Mayor Mascone and Harvey Milk were assassinated and the gay community rioted, yet had no awareness of these events. Another lived in New York City, yet still had never met a gay or lesbian person in high school. I think that this is a very important finding because it sets the experiences of gay and lesbian youth apart from the experiences of gay and lesbian adults. I would argue that although life for gay and lesbian adults has changed a great deal in the last thirty years, it has changed very little for gay and lesbian youth. I think that the experiences of a gay or lesbian high schooler in Catholic schools in 2000 are about the same in most cases as those of a gay or lesbian high schooler in Catholic school in 1969, and maybe even 1959.

Do Catholic high schools help their students see sexuality as "a fundamental component of personality," as something integrated into their identity? Are they able to see themselves as whole persons with their sexuality? The stories from my study show dis-integration at a fundamental level, the level of identity.

Chapter 7

Conclusion

Given the stories presented here, what should Catholic high schools do to better serve gay and lesbian students? I wish answers were easy. The difficulty is that very little has been done; much is left to speculation. Some Catholic schools have begun to address the issue. In the Archdiocese of St. Paul, Minnesota, Catholic high schools have begun to train their faculties on the issue and have started to discuss homosexuality with their students (Gevelinger and Zimmerman, 1997). It will take many brave efforts such as these, and the study of these efforts, to initiate progress. Most important, the silence on this topic must be broken.

I wish to rely on the last paragraph of the American bishops statement (United States Catholic Conference, 1991) to make some recommendations. The bishops stress, first of all, that the topic cannot be ignored. Catholic high schools must create an atmosphere in which homosexuality can be discussed. It must be presented in classrooms, in counselors' offices, in liturgy, and integrated throughout the life of the school in context with other social justice topics. In their 1997 statement, the American Bishops' Committee on Marriage and Family has recommended that AIDS be introduced in the petitions at liturgies. My hope is that we can go even further with this to include a whole variety of issues related to gay and lesbian people.

The bishops also stress, "First and foremost, we support modeling and teaching respect for every human person, regardless of sexual orientation" (United States Catholic Conference, 1991, p. 56). Is this message "first and foremost" in the minds of most people, including gay and lesbian students, when they think of the Church's teaching on homosexuality? Although it would be the subject of another study, I think that what comes to mind for most people when they hear "the Catholic Church's teaching on homosexuality" is the Church's condemnations of homosexual activity, not the dignity and worth of the human person. Wouldn't it be wonderful if this were "first and foremost" in people's minds? This *must* be the primary message communicated in Catholic high schools.

"Second, a parent or teacher must also present clearly and delicately the unambiguous moral norms of the Christian tradition regarding homosexual genital activity" (United States Catholic Conference, 1991, p. 56). I wish to emphasize that this message is "second." If the sex education in a Catholic high school already emphasizes that sexual activity is only appropriate for persons in marriage (a safe assumption) this point has already been made and needs no further clarification. This should never be the only thing or even the primary thing said about homosexuality in a Catholic high school. It must also be remembered that individual acts of homosexual sex are to be judged with prudence.

The bishops also point out that parents and educators must be open to the possibility that an adolescent is struggling to accept his or her own homosexual orientation. The struggle for self-acceptance is discussed in Chapter 6. Identity dis-integration is the experience of gay and lesbian students in Catholic high schools. Catholic high schools must work to integrate a student's homosexuality into his or her identity. As with all of Catholic education, this involves an integrated approach. Home, social groups, curriculum, and spirituality will need to be involved for this to take place.

Finally, a very delicate point. The bishops state, "The distinction between *being* homosexual and *doing* homosexual genital actions, while not always clear and convincing, is a helpful and important one when dealing with the complex issue of homosexuality, particularly in the educational and pastoral arena." The Church's condemnations of homosexual activity must not prevent those working for the Church from providing pastoral care for homosexual persons.

I wish to mention here the "not always clear and convincing" issue. I have been very careful throughout this book to provide unquestionable sources from the Catholic hierarchy. I wish to give people working in Catholic education some "ammo" to deal with those who say, "But how can you do this in a *Catholic* school?" I want people to be able to better serve gay and lesbian students in Catholic high schools *because* these are Catholic schools, not despite that. I do feel compelled, however, to raise the issue of dis-integration within the Church's teaching itself. Is it possible in the minds of most people to believe that it is not sinful to be gay or lesbian but it is sinful to have gay or lesbian sex in all situations, even those of loving committed relationships? Can most people defend the rights of gay and lesbian people and at the same time condemn the actions they take in expressing love?

In my 1995 survey study, I found that most adolescents cannot hold both of these views simultaneously. The first two statements on the survey are negative about homosexuality; "Homosexuality is a disorder," and "Sexual acts between persons of the same sex are morally wrong." The other fourteen statements are positive. They affirm the rights of gay and lesbian people and the Church's responsibility to minister to them. I found a correlation of $-.653$ between responses on the first two items and responses on the rest of the survey in the 1995 study. What this means, in short, is that if a student agreed with the first two items, he or she was not likely to agree with the rest of them. The reverse is also true. Most people agree with either one part of the Church's teaching or another, not both parts. Almost all of the counselors interviewed made a point of telling me that they disagreed with the Church's condemnations of homosexuality sexual activity. The only counselor who told me he agreed with the Church's condemnations was Father Morgan. His own story in Chapter 6 makes this even more worrisome. I hope for the day when not only are our gay and lesbian students integrated but so too is the teaching of our magisterium.

Appendix A

Statements from the Catholic Magisterium

Statement from the United States Catholic Conference, *Human Sexuality: A Catholic Perspective for Education and Lifelong Learning,* 1991, pp. 54-56

Sexuality, as noted earlier, is a fundamental dimension of every human being. It is reflected physiologically, psychologically, and relationally in a person's gender identity as well as in one's primary sexual orientation and behavior. For some young men and women, this means a discovery that one is homosexual, that is, that one's "sexual inclinations are oriented predominantly toward persons of the same sex."[45] Other persons experience a bisexual orientation. These orientations involve one's feelings and sexual fantasies as well as one's overtly sexual and genital actions.

In recent decades, a distinction has been drawn between persons whose homosexual orientation seems to be transitory—the result of education, environment, or adolescent habit—and those persons for whom homosexuality is a permanent, seemingly irreversible sexual orientation. The medical and behavioral sciences do not as yet know what causes a person to be homosexual. Whether it is related to genetics, hormones, or some variation in psychosocial upbringing, the scientific data presently seems inconclusive. There may be a combination of factors involved.

Mindful of the inherent and abiding dignity of every human person, we affirm what we wrote in 1976, namely, that "homosexual [persons], like everyone else, should not suffer from prejudice against their basic human rights. They have a right to respect, friendship, and justice. They should have an active role in the Christian community."[46] We echo strongly the Congregation for the Doctrine of the Faith, which, in a 1986 document stated, "It is deplorable that homosexual persons have been and are the object of violent malice in speech or in action. Such treatment deserves condemnation from the Church's pastors wherever it occurs."[47]

We call on all Christians and citizens of good will to confront their own fears about homosexuality and to curb the humor and discrimination that offend homosexual persons. We understand that having a homosexual orientation brings with it enough anxiety, pain, and issues related to self-acceptance without society adding additional prejudicial treatment.

However, we also want to express clearly the Church's teaching that "homosexual [genital] activity, as distinguished from homosexual orientation, is morally wrong."[48] Such an orientation in itself, because not freely chosen, is not sinful.[49] As we have stated several times in this document, we believe that it is only within a heterosexual marital relationship that genital sexual activity is morally acceptable. Only within marriage does sexual intercourse fully symbolize the Creator's dual design, as an act of covenant love, with the potential of co-creating new human life. Therefore, homosexual genital activity is considered immoral. Like heterosexual persons, homosexual men and women are called to give witness to chastity, avoiding, with God's grace, behavior that is wrong for them, just as non-marital sexual relations are wrong for heterosexual men and women.[50]

In the pastoral field, we affirm that homosexual men and women "must certainly be treated with understanding"and sustained in Christian hope.[51] Their moral responsibility ought to be judged with a degree of prudence. Parents, teachers, confessors, and the whole "Christian community should offer a special degree of pastoral understanding and care," particularly since having a homosexual orientation generally precludes a person from entering marriage.[52]

Living as a chaste homosexual is not an easy way of life, particularly if one feels drawn to live a commitment with another person. The Church challenges homosexual men and women to join "whatever sufferings and difficulties they experience in virtue of their condition to the sacrifice of the Lord's cross."[53] This is not to be seen merely as pointless self-denial. Rather, following the way of the cross is the way of virtue, of becoming a mature, sexually appropriate, chaste person, in service to the will of God.

Educationally, homosexuality cannot and ought not to be skirted or ignored. The topic "must be faced in all objectivity by the pupil and the educator when the case presents itself."[54] First and foremost, we support modeling and teaching respect for every human person, regardless of sexual orientation. Second, a parent or teacher must also present clearly and delicately the unambiguous moral norms of the Christian tradition regarding homosexual genital activity, appropriately geared to the age level and maturity of the learner. Finally, parents and other educators must remain open to the possibility that a particular person, whether adolescent or adult, may be struggling to accept his or her own homosexual orientation. The distinction between *being* homosexual and *doing* homosexual genital actions, while not always clear and convincing, is a helpful and important one when dealing with the complex issue of homosexuality, particularly in the educational and pastoral arena.

Notes

45. National Conference of Catholic Bishops, *Principles to Guide Confessors in Questions of Homosexuality* (Washington, DC: USCC Office for Publishing and Promotion Services, 1973), p. 3.

46. *To Live in Christ Jesus*, no. 52.

47. *Letter to the Bishops of the Catholic Church on the Pastoral Care of Homosexual Persons*, no. 10.

48. *To Live in Christ Jesus*, no. 52.

49. See *Letter to the Bishops of the Catholic Church on the Pastoral Care of Homosexual Persons*, no. 3: "Although the particular inclination of the homosexual person is not a sin, it is a more or less strong tendency ordered toward an intrinsic moral evil; and thus the inclination itself must be seen as an objective disorder." Here, two things must be noted. To speak of the homosexual *inclination* as "objectively disordered" does not mean that the homosexual *person* as such is evil or bad. Furthermore, the homosexual person is not the only one who has disordered tendencies or inclinations. All human beings are subject to some disordered tendencies.

50. See *To Live in Christ Jesus*, no. 52.

51. See *Declaration on Certain Questions Concerning Sexual Ethics*, no. 8.

52. *To Live in Christ Jesus*, no. 52.

53. *Letter to the Bishops of the Catholic Church on the Pastoral Care of Homosexual Persons*, no. 12.

54. *Educational Guidance in Human Love*, no. 101.

**Statement from the United States Catholic Conference,
NCCB Committee on Marriage and Family,**
*Always Our Children: Pastoral Message
to Parents of Homosexual Children
and Suggestions for Pastoral Ministers,* **1997**

PREFACE

The purpose of this pastoral message is to reach out to parents who are trying to cope with the discovery of homosexuality in their adolescent or adult child. It urges families to draw upon the reservoirs of faith, hope, and love as they face uncharted futures. It asks them to recognize that the Church offers enormous spiritual resources to strengthen and support them at this moment in their family's life and in the days to come.

This message draws upon the *Catechism of the Catholic Church,* the teachings of Pope John Paul II, and statements of the Congregation for the Doctrine of the Faith and of our own conference. This message is not a treatise on homosexuality. It is not a systematic presentation of the Church's moral teaching. It does not break any new ground theologically. Rather, relying on the Church's teaching, as well as on our own pastoral experience, we intend to speak words of faith, hope, and love to parents who need the Church's loving presence at a time that may be one of the most challenging in their lives. We also hope this message will be helpful to priests and pastoral ministers who often are the first ones parents or their children approach with their struggles and anxieties.

In recent years, we have tried to reach out to families in difficult circumstances. Our initiatives took the form of short statements, like this one, addressed to people who thought they were beyond the Church's circle of care. *Always Our Children* follows in the same tradition.

This message is not intended for advocacy purposes or to serve a particular agenda. It is not to be understood as an endorsement of what some call a "homosexual lifestyle." *Always Our Children* is an outstretched hand of the bishop's Committee on Marriage and Family to parents and other family members, offering them a fresh look at the grace present in family life and the unfailing mercy of Christ our Lord.

> *"An even more generous, intelligent and prudent pastoral commitment modeled on the Good Shepherd is called for in cases of families which, often independently of their own wishes and through pressures of various other kinds, find themselves faced by situations which are objectively difficult."* --Pope John Paul II, On the Family, *1981, no. 77.*

A Critical Moment, A Time of Grace

As you begin to read this message you may feel that your life is in turmoil. You and your family might be faced with one of the difficult situations of which our Holy Father speaks:

—You think your adolescent child is experiencing a same-sex attraction and/or you observe attitudes and behaviors that you find confusing or upsetting or with which you disagree.

—Your son or daughter has made it known that he or she has a homosexual orientation.

—You experience a tension between loving your child as God's precious creation and not wanting to endorse any behavior you know the Church teaches is wrong.

You need not face this painful time alone, without human assistance or God's grace. The Church can be an instrument of both help and healing. This is why we bishops, as pastors and teachers, write to you.

In this pastoral message, we draw upon the gift of faith as well as the sound teaching and pastoral practice of the Church in order to offer loving support, reliable guidance, and recommendations for ministries suited to your needs and to those of your child. Our message speaks of accepting yourself, your beliefs and values, your questions, and all you may be struggling with at this moment; accepting and loving your child as a gift of God; and accepting the full truth of God's revelation about the dignity of the human person and the meaning of human sexuality. Within the Catholic moral vision there is no contradiction among these levels of acceptance, for truth and love are not opposed. They are inseparably joined and rooted in one person, Jesus Christ, who reveals God to be ultimate truth and saving love.

We address our message also to the wider church community, and especially to priests and other pastoral ministers, asking that our words be translated into attitudes and actions which follow the way of love, as Christ has taught. It is through the community of his faithful that Jesus offers hope, help and healing so that your whole family might continue to grow into the intimate community of life and love that God intends.

Accepting Yourself

Because some of you might be swept up in a tide of emotions, we focus first on feelings. Although the gift of human sexuality can be a great mystery at times, the Church's teaching on homosexuality is clear. However, because the terms of that teaching have now become very personal in regard to your son or daughter, you may feel confused and conflicted.

You could be experiencing many different emotions, all in varying degrees, such as the following:

Relief: Perhaps you had sensed for some time that your son or daughter was different in some way. Now he or she has come to you and has entrusted something very significant. It may be that other siblings learned of this before you and were reluctant to tell you. Regardless, though, a burden has been lifted. Acknowledge the possibility that your child has told you this not to hurt you or create distance, but out of love and trust and with a desire for honesty, intimacy, and closer communication.

Anger: You may be feeling deceived or manipulated by your son or daughter. You could be angry with your spouse, blaming him or her for "making the child this way"—especially if there has been a difficult parent-child relationship. You might be angry with yourself for not recognizing indications of homosexuality. You could be feeling disappointment, along with anger, if family members, and sometimes even siblings, are rejecting their homosexual brother or sister. It is just as possible to feel anger if family members or friends seem overly accepting and encouraging of homosexuality. Also—and not to be discounted—is a possible anger with God that all this is happening.

Mourning: You may now feel that your child is not exactly the same individual you once thought you knew. You envision that your son or daughter may never give you grandchildren. These lost expectations as well as the fact that homosexual persons often encounter discrimination and open hostility can cause you great sadness.

Fear: You may fear for your child's physical safety and general welfare in the face of prejudice against homosexual people. In particular, you may be afraid that others in your community might exclude or treat your child or your family with contempt. The fear of your child contracting HIV/AIDS or another sexually transmitted disease is serious and ever present. If your child is distraught, you may be concerned about attempted suicide.

Guilt, Shame, and Loneliness: "If only we had . . . or had not . . ." are words with which parents can torture themselves at this stage. Regrets and disappointments rise up like ghosts from the past. A sense of failure can lead you into a valley of shame which, in turn, can isolate you from your children, your family, and other communities of support.

Parental Protectiveness and Pride: Homosexual persons often experience discrimination and acts of violence in our society. As a parent, you naturally want to shield your children from harm, regardless of their age. You may still insist: "You are always my child; nothing can ever change that. You are also a child of God, gifted and called for a purpose in God's design."

There are two important things to keep in mind as you try to sort out your feelings. First, listen to them. They can contain clues leading to a fuller discovery of God's will for you. Second, because some feelings can be confusing or conflicting, it is not necessary to act upon all of them. Acknowledging them may be sufficient, but it may also be necessary to talk about your feelings. Do not expect that all tensions can or will be resolved. The Christian life is a journey marked by perseverance and prayer. It is a path leading from where we are to where we know God is calling us.

Accepting Your Child

How can you best express your love—itself a reflection of God's unconditional love—for your child? At least two things are necessary.

First, don't break off contact; don't reject your child. A shocking number of homosexual youth end up on the streets because of rejection by their families. This, and other external pressures, can place young people at a greater risk for self-destructive behaviors like substance abuse and suicide.

Your child may need you and the family now more than ever. He or she is still the same person. This child, who has always been God's gift to you, may now be the cause of another gift: your family becoming more honest, respectful, and supportive. Yes, your love can be tested by this reality, but it can also grow stronger through your struggle to respond lovingly.

The second way to communicate love is to seek appropriate help for your child and for yourself. If your son or daughter is an adolescent, it is possible that he or she may be displaying traits which cause you anxiety such as what the child is choosing to read or view in the media, intense friendships, and other such observable characteristics and tendencies. What is called for on the part of parents is an approach which does not presume that your child has developed a homosexual orientation, and which will help you maintain a loving relationship while you provide support, information, encouragement, and moral guidance. Parents must always be vigilant about their children's behavior and exercise responsible interventions when necessary.

In many cases, it may be appropriate and necessary that your child receive professional help, including counseling and spiritual direction. It is important, of course, that he or she receive such guidance willingly. Look for a therapist who has an appreciation of religious values and who understands the complex nature of sexuality. Such a person should be experienced at helping people discern the meaning of early sexual behaviors, sexual attractions, and sexual fantasies in ways that lead to more clarity and self-identity. In the course of this, however, it is essential for you to remain open to the possibility that your son or daughter is struggling to understand and accept a basic homosexual orientation.

The meaning and implications of the term homosexual orientation are not universally agreed upon. Church teaching acknowledges a distinction between homosexual "tendency" which proves to be "transitory" and "homosexuals who are definitively such because of some kind of innate instinct" (Congregation for the Doctrine of the Faith, *Declaration on Certain Questions Concerning Sexual Ethics,* 8).

In light of this possibility, therefore, it seems appropriate to understand sexual orientation (heterosexual or homosexual) as a deepseated dimension of one's personality and to recognize its relative stability in a person. A homosexual orientation produces a stronger emotional and sexual attraction toward individuals of the same sex, rather than toward those of the opposite sex. It does not totally rule out interest in, care for, and attraction toward members of the opposite sex. Having a homosexual orientation does not necessarily mean a person will engage in homosexual activity.

There seems to be no single cause of a homosexual orientation. A common opinion of experts is that there are multiple factors—genetic, hormonal, psychological—that may give rise to it. Generally, homosexual orientation is experienced as a given, not as something freely chosen. By itself, therefore, a homosexual orientation cannot be considered sinful, for morality presumes the freedom to choose.[1]

Some homosexual persons want to be known publicly as gay or lesbian. These terms often express a person's level of self-awareness and self-acceptance within society. Though you might find the terms offensive because of political or social connotations, it is necessary to be sensitive to how your son or daughter is using them. Language should not be a barrier to building trust and honest communication.

You can help a homosexual person in two general ways. First, encourage him or her to cooperate with God's grace to live a chaste life. Second, concentrate on the person, not on the homosexual orientation itself. This implies respecting a person's freedom to choose or refuse therapy directed toward changing a homosexual orientation. Given the present state of medical and psychological knowledge, there is no guarantee that such therapy will succeed. Thus, there may be no obligation to undertake it, though some may find it helpful.

All in all, it is essential to recall one basic truth. God loves every person as a unique individual. Sexual identity helps to define the unique persons we are, and one component of our sexual identity is sexual orientation. Thus, our total personhood is more encompassing than sexual orientation. Human beings see the appearance, but the Lord looks into the heart (cf. 1 Samuel 16.7).

God does not love someone any less simply because he or she is homosexual. God's love is always and everywhere offered to those who are open to receiving it. St. Paul's words offer great hope:

"For I am convinced that neither death, nor life, nor angels, nor principalities, nor present things, nor future things, nor powers, nor height, nor depth, nor any other creature will be able to separate us from the love of God in Christ Jesus our Lord" (Romans 8.38-39).

Accepting God's Plan and the Church's Ministry

For the Christian believer, an acceptance of self and of one's homosexual child must take place within the larger context of accepting divinely revealed truth about the dignity and destiny of human persons. It is the Church's responsibility to believe and teach this truth, presenting it as a comprehensive moral vision and applying this vision in particular situations through its pastoral ministries. We present the main points of that moral teaching here.

Every person has an inherent dignity because he or she is created in God's image. A deep respect for the total person leads the Church to hold and teach that sexuality is a gift from God. Being created a male or female person is an essential part of the divine plan, for it is their sexuality—a mysterious blend of spirit and body—that allows human beings to share in God's own creative love and life.

Like all gifts from God, the power and freedom of sexuality can be channeled toward good or evil. Everyone—the homosexual and the heterosexual person—is called to personal maturity and responsibility. With the help of God's grace, everyone is called to practice the virtue of chastity in relationships. Chastity means integrating one's thoughts, feelings, and actions, in the area of human sexuality, in a way that values and respects one's own dignity and that of others. It is "the spiritual power which frees love from selfishness and aggression" (Pontifical Council for the Family, *The Truth and Meaning of Human Sexuality,* 16).

Christ summons all his followers—whether they are married or living a single celibate life—to a higher standard of loving. This includes not only fidelity, forgiveness, hope, perseverance, and sacrifice, but also chastity, which is expressed in modesty and self-control. The chaste life is possible, though not always easy, for it involves a continual effort to turn toward God and away from sin, especially with the strength of the sacraments of penance and eucharist. Indeed God expects everyone to strive for the perfection of love, but to achieve it gradually through stages of moral growth (cf. John Paul II, *On the Family,* 34). To keep our feet on the path of conversion, God's grace is available to and sufficient for everyone open to receiving it.

Furthermore, as homosexual persons "dedicate their lives to understanding the nature of God's personal call to them, they will be able to celebrate the sacrament of penance more faithfully and receive the Lord's grace so freely offered there in order to convert their lives more fully this way" (Congregation for the Doctrine of the Faith, *Letter on the Pastoral Care of Homosexual Persons,* 1986, no. 12).

To live and love chastely is to understand that "only within marriage does sexual intercourse fully symbolize the Creator's dual design, as an act of covenant love, with the potential of co-creating new human life" (U.S. Catholic Conference, *Human Sexuality: A Catholic Perspective for Education and Lifelong Learning,* p. 55). This is a fundamental teaching of our Church about sexuality, rooted in the biblical account of man and woman created in the image of God and made for union with one another (Genesis 2-3).

Two conclusions follow. First, it is God's plan that sexual intercourse occur only within marriage between a man and a woman. Second, every act of intercourse must be open to the possible creation of human life. Homosexual intercourse cannot fulfill these two conditions. Therefore, the Church teaches that homogenital behavior is objectively immoral, while making the important distinction between this behavior and a homosexual orientation, which is not immoral in itself. It is also important to recognize that neither a homosexual orientation, nor a heterosexual one, leads inevitably to sexual activity. One's total personhood is not reducible to sexual orientation or behavior.

Respect for the God-given dignity of all persons means the recognition of human rights and responsibilities. The teachings of the Church make it clear that the fundamental human rights of homosexual persons must be defended and that all of us must strive to eliminate any forms of injustice, oppression, or violence against them (cf. Congregation for the Doctrine of the Faith, *The Pastoral Care of Homosexual Persons,* 1986, no.10).

It is not sufficient only to avoid unjust discrimination. Homosexual persons "must be accepted with respect, compassion and sensitivity" (*Catechism of the Catholic Church,* 2358). They, as is true of every human being, need to be nourished at many different levels simultaneously. This includes friendship, which is a way of loving and is essential to healthy human development. It is one of the richest possible human experiences. Friendship can and does thrive outside of genital sexual involvement.

The Christian community should offer its homosexual sisters and brothers understanding and pastoral care. More than twenty years ago, we bishops stated that "Homosexuals . . . should have an active role in the Christian community" (National Conference of Catholic Bishops, *To Live in Christ Jesus: A Pastoral Reflection on the Moral Life,* p. 19). What does this mean in practice? It means that all homosexual persons have a right to be welcomed into the community, to hear the word of God, and to receive pastoral care. Homosexual persons living chaste lives should have opportunities to lead and serve the community. However, the Church has the right to deny public roles of service and leadership to persons, whether homosexual or heterosexual, whose public behavior openly violates its teachings.

The Church also recognizes the importance and urgency of ministering to persons with HIV/AIDS. Though HIV/AIDS is an epidemic affecting the whole human race, not just homosexual persons, it has had a devastating effect upon them and has brought great sorrow to many parents, families, and friends.

Without condoning self-destructive behavior or denying personal responsibility, we reject the idea that HIV/AIDS is a direct punishment from God. Furthermore:

"Persons with AIDS are not distant, unfamiliar people, the objects of our mingled pity and aversion. We must keep them present to our consciousness as individuals and a community, and embrace them with unconditional love. . . . Compassion—love—toward persons infected with HIV is the only authentic Gospel response" (National Conference of Catholic Bishops, *Called to Compassion and Responsibility: A Response to the HIV/AIDS Crisis,* 1989).

Nothing in the Bible or in Catholic teaching can be used to justify prejudicial or discriminatory attitudes and behaviors.[2] We reiterate here what we said in an earlier statement:

"We call on all Christians and citizens of good will to confront their own fears about homosexuality and to curb the humor and discrimination that offend homosexual persons. We understand that having a homosexual orientation brings with it enough anxiety, pain and issues related to self-acceptance without society bringing additional prejudicial treatment" (*Human Sexuality: A Catholic Perspective for Education and Lifelong Learning,* p. 55).

Pastoral Recommendations

With a view toward overcoming isolation that you or your son or daughter may be experiencing, we offer these recommendations to you as well as to priests and pastoral ministers.

To Parents:
1. Accept and love yourselves as parents in order to accept and love your son or daughter. Do not blame yourselves for a homosexual orientation in your child.

2. Do everything possible to continue demonstrating love for your child. However, accepting his or her homosexual orientation does not have to include approving all related attitudes and behavioral choices. In fact, you may need to challenge certain aspects of a lifestyle that you find objectionable.

3. Urge your son or daughter to stay joined to the Catholic faith community. If they have left the Church, urge them to return and be

reconciled to the community, especially through the sacrament of penance.

4. Recommend that your son or daughter find a spiritual director/mentor to offer guidance in prayer and in leading a chaste and virtuous life.

5. Seek help for yourself, perhaps in the form of counseling or spiritual direction, as you strive for understanding, acceptance, and inner peace. Also, consider joining a parents' support group or participating in a retreat designed for Catholic parents of homosexual children. Other people have traveled the same road as you but may have journeyed even further. They can share effective ways of handling delicate family situations such as how to tell family members and friends about your child, how to explain homosexuality to younger children, and how to relate to your son or daughter's friends in a Christian way.

6. Reach out in love and service to other parents who may be struggling with a son or daughter's homosexuality. Contact your parish about organizing a parents' support group. Your diocesan family ministry office, Catholic Charities, or a special diocesan ministry to gay and lesbian persons may be able to offer assistance.

7. As you take advantage of opportunities for education and support, remember that you can only change yourself; you can only be responsible for your own beliefs and actions, not those of your adult children.

8. Put your faith completely in God, who is more powerful, more compassionate, and more forgiving than we are or could ever be.

To Church Ministers:

1. Be available to parents and families who ask for your pastoral help, spiritual guidance, and prayer.

2. Welcome homosexual persons into the faith community, and seek out those on the margins. Avoid stereotyping and condemnations. Strive first to listen. Do not presume that all homosexual persons are sexually active.

3. Learn more about homosexuality and church teaching so your preaching, teaching, and counseling will be informed and effective.

4. When speaking publicly, use the words "homosexual," "gay," and "lesbian" in honest and accurate ways.

5. Maintain a list of agencies, community groups, and counselors or other experts to whom you can refer homosexual persons or their

parents and family members when they ask you for specialized assistance. Recommend agencies that operate in a manner consistent with Catholic teaching.

6. Help to establish or promote existing support groups for parents and family members.

7. Learn about HIV/AIDS so you will be more informed and compassionate in your ministry. Include prayers in the liturgy for those living with HIV/AIDS, their caregivers, those who have died, and their families, companions, and friends. A special Mass for healing and anointing of the sick might be connected with World AIDS Awareness Day (Dec. 1) or with a local AIDS awareness program.

CONCLUSION

For St. Paul love is the greatest of spiritual gifts. St. John considers love to be the most certain sign of God's presence. Jesus proposes it as the basis of his two great commandments which fulfill all the law and the prophets.

Love, too, is the continuing story of every family's life. Love can be shared, nurtured, rejected, and sometimes lost. To follow Christ's way of love is the challenge before every family today. Your family now has an added opportunity to share love and to accept love. Our church communities are likewise called to an exemplary standard of love and justice. Our homosexual sisters and brothers—indeed, all people—are summoned into responsible ways of loving.

To our homosexual brothers and sisters we offer a concluding word. This message has been an outstretched hand to your parents and families inviting them to accept God's grace present in their lives now and to trust in the unfailing mercy of Jesus our Lord. Now we stretch out our hands and invite you to do the same. We are called to become one body, one spirit in Christ. We need one another if we are to ". . . grow in every way into him who is the head, Christ, from whom the whole body, joined and held together by every supporting ligament, with the proper functioning of each part, brings about the body's growth and builds itself up in love" (Ephesians 4. 15-16).

Though at times you may feel discouraged, hurt, or angry, do not walk away from your families, from the Christian community, from all those who love you. In you God's love is revealed. You are always our children.

> "There is no fear in love . . . perfect love drives out fear" (1 John 4.18).

Notes

1. The *Catechism of the Catholic Church* states also: "This inclination, which is objectively disordered, constitutes for most [persons with the homosexual inclination] a trial" (no. 2358).

2. In matters where sexual orientation has a clear relevance, the common good does justify its being taken into account, as noted by the Congregation for the Doctrine of the Faith in *Some Considerations Concerning the Response to Legislative Proposals on the Non-Discrimination of Homosexual Persons*, 1992, no. 11.

Always Our Children: Pastoral Message to Parents of Homosexual Children and Suggestions for Pastoral Ministers is a statement of the NCCB Committee on Marriage and Family. It was prepared in the Secretariat for Family, Laity, Women, and Youth under the supervision of the above committee. Publication was approved by the Administrative Committee on September 10, 1997. The statement is further authorized for publication by the undersigned.
Monsignor Dennis M. Schnurr, General Secretary, NCCB/USCC

Statement from the Vatican Congregation for the Doctrine of the Faith, *Letter to the Bishops of the Catholic Church on the Pastoral Care of Homosexual Persons*, 1986

1. The issue of homosexuality and the moral evaluation of homosexual acts have increasingly become a matter of public debate, even in Catholic circles. Since this debate often advances arguments and makes assertions inconsistent with the teachings of the Catholic Church, it is quite rightly a cause for concern to all engaged in the pastoral ministry, and this congregation has judged it to be of sufficiently grave and widespread importance to address to the bishops of the Catholic Church this letter on the pastoral care of homosexual persons.

2. Naturally, an exhaustive treatment of this complex issue cannot be attempted here, but we will focus our reflection within the distinc-

tive context of the Catholic moral perspective. It is a perspective which finds support in the more secure findings of the natural sciences, which have their own legitimate and proper methodology and field of inquiry.

However, the Catholic moral viewpoint is founded on human reason illuminated by faith and is consciously motivated by the desire to do the will of God, our Father. The Church is thus in a position to learn from scientific discovery but also to transcend the horizons of science and to be confident that her more global vision does greater justice to the rich reality of the human person in his spiritual and physical dimensions created by God and heir, by grace, to eternal life.

It is within this context, then, that it can be clearly seen that the phenomenon of homosexuality, complex as it is and with its many consequences for society and ecclesial life, is a proper focus for the Church's pastoral care. It thus requires of her ministers attentive study, active concern and honest, theologically well-balanced counsel.

3. Explicit treatment of the problem was given in this congregation's "Declaration on Certain Questions Concerning Sexual Ethics" of Dec. 29, 1975. That document stressed the duty of trying to understand the homosexual condition and noted that culpability for homosexual acts should be judged with prudence. At the same time the congregation took note of the distinction commonly drawn between the homosexual condition or tendency and individual homosexual actions. These were described as deprived of their essential and indispensable finality, as being "intrinsically disordered" and able in no case to be approved of (cf. No. 8).

In the discussion which followed the publication of the declaration, however, an overly benign interpretation was given to the homosexual condition itself, some going so far as to call it neutral or even good. Although the particular inclination of the homosexual person is not a sin, it is a more or less strong tendency ordered toward an intrinsic moral evil and thus the inclination itself must be seen as an objective disorder.

Therefore special concern and pastoral attention should be directed toward those who have this condition, lest they be led to believe that the living out of this orientation in homosexual activity is a morally acceptable option. It is not.

4. An essential dimension of authentic pastoral care is the identification of causes of confusion regarding the Church's teaching. One is a new exegesis of Sacred Scripture which claims variously that Scripture has nothing to say on the subject of homosexuality or that it somehow tacitly approves of it or that all of its moral injunctions are so culture-bound that they are no longer applicable to contemporary life. These views are gravely erroneous and call for particular attention here.

5. It is quite true that the biblical literature owes to the different epochs in which it was written a good deal of its varied patterns of thought and expression (*Dei Verbum,* 12). The Church today addresses the Gospel to a world which differs in many ways from ancient days. But the world in which the New Testament was written was already quite diverse from the situation in which the Sacred Scriptures of the Hebrew people had been written or compiled, for example.

What should be noticed is that in the presence of such remarkable diversity there is nevertheless a clear consistency within the Scriptures themselves on the moral issue of homosexual behavior. The Church's doctrine regarding this issue is based not on isolated phrases for facile theological argument, but on the solid foundation of a constant biblical testimony. The community of faith today, in unbroken continuity with Jewish and Christian communities within which the ancient Scriptures were written, continues to be nourished by those same Scriptures and by the Spirit of Truth whose word they are. It is likewise essential to recognize that the Scriptures are not properly understood when they are interpreted in a way which contradicts the Church's living tradition. To be correct, the interpretation of Scripture must be in substantial accord with that tradition.

Vatican Council II in *Dei Verbum,* No. 10, put it this way: "It is clear, therefore, that in the supremely wise arrangement of God, sacred tradition, Sacred Scripture and the magisterium of the Church are so connected and associated that one of them cannot stand without the others. Working together, each in its own way under the action of the one Holy Sprit, they all contribute effectively to the salvation of souls." In that spirit we wish to outline briefly the biblical teaching here.

6. Providing a basic plan for understanding this entire discussion of homosexuality is the theology of creation we find in Genesis. God, by his infinite wisdom and love, brings into existence all of reality as a reflection of his goodness. He fashions mankind, male and female, in his own image and likeness. Human beings, therefore, are nothing less that the work of God himself and in the complementarity of the sexes they are called to reflect the inner unity of the Creator. They do this in a striking way in their cooperation with him in the transmission of life by a mutual donation of the self to the other.

In Genesis 3, we find that this truth about persons being an image of God has been obscured by original sin. There inevitably follows a loss of awareness of the covenental character of the union these persons had with God and with each other. The human body retains its "spousal significance," but this is now clouded by sin. Thus, in Genesis 19.1-11, the deterioration due to sin continues in the story of the men of Sodom. There can be no doubt of the moral judgment made there against homosexual relations. In Leviticus 18.22 and 20.13, in the course of describing the conditions necessary for belonging to the chosen people, the author excludes from the people of God those who behave in a homosexual fashion.

Against the background of this exposition of theocratic law, an eschatological perspective is developed by St. Paul when, in 1 Corinthians 6.9, he proposes the same doctrine and lists those who behave in a homosexual fashion among those who shall not enter the kingdom of God.

In Romans 1.18-32, still building on the moral traditions of his forebears but in the new context of confrontation between Christianity and the pagan society of his day, Paul uses homosexual behavior as an example of the blindness which has overcome humankind. Instead of the original harmony between Creator and creatures, the acute distortion of idolatry has led to all kinds of moral excess. Paul is at a loss to find a clearer example of this disharmony than homosexual relations. Finally, 1 Timothy 1, in full continuity with the biblical position, singles out those who spread wrong doctrine and in Verse 10 explicitly names as sinners those who engage in homosexual acts.

7. The Church, obedient to the Lord who founded her and gave to her the sacramental life, celebrates the divine plan of the loving and life-giving union of men and women in the sacrament of marriage. It is only in the marital relationship that the use of the sexual facility can

be morally good. A person engaged in homosexual behavior therefore acts immorally.

To choose someone of the same sex for one's sexual activity is to annul the rich symbolism and meaning, not to mention the goals, of the Creator's sexual design. Homosexual activity is not a complimentary union able to transmit life; and so it thwarts the call to a life of that form of self-giving which the Gospel says is the essence of Christian living. This does not mean that homosexual persons are not often generous and giving of themselves; but when they engage in homosexual activity they confirm within themselves a disordered sexual inclination which is essentially self-indulgent.

As in every moral disorder, homosexual activity prevents one's own fulfillment and happiness by acting contrary to the creative wisdom of God. The Church, in rejecting erroneous opinions regarding homosexuality, does not limit but rather defends personal freedom and dignity realistically and authentically understood.

8. Thus, the Church's teaching today is in organic continuity with the scriptural perspective and with her own constant tradition. Though today's world is in many ways quite new, the Christian community senses the profound and lasting bonds which join us to those generations who have gone before us, "marked with the sign of faith."

Nevertheless, increasing numbers of people today, even within the Church, are bringing enormous pressure to bear on the Church to accept the homosexual condition as though it were not disordered and to condone homosexual activity. Those within the Church who argue in this fashion often have close ties with those with similar views outside it. These later groups are guided by a vision opposed to the truth about the human person, which is fully disclosed in the mystery of Christ. They reflect, even if not entirely consciously, a materialistic ideology which denies the transcendent nature of the human person as well as the supernatural vocation of every individual.

The Church's ministers must ensure that homosexual persons in their care will not be misled by this point of view, so profoundly opposed to the teaching of the Church. But the risk is great, and there are many who seek to create confusion regarding the Church's position and then to use that confusion to their own advantage.

9. The movement within the Church, which takes the form of pressure groups of various names and sizes, attempts to give the impression

that it represents all homosexual persons who are Catholics. As a matter of fact, its membership by and large is restricted to those who either ignore the teaching of the Church or who seek somehow to undermine it. It brings together under the aegis of Catholicism homosexual persons who have no intention of abandoning their homosexual behavior. One tactic used is to protest that any and all criticisms of or reservations about homosexual people, their activity and lifestyle are simply diverse forms of unjust discrimination.

There is an effort in some countries to manipulate the Church by gaining the often well-intentioned support of her pastors with a view to changing civil statues and laws. This is done in order to conform to these pressure groups' concept that homosexuality is at least a completely harmless, if not an entirely good, thing. Even when the practice of homosexuality may seriously threaten the lives and well-being of a large number of people, its advocates remain undeterred and refuse to consider the magnitude of the risks involved.

The Church can never be so callous. It is true that her clear position cannot be revised by pressure from civil legislation or the trend of the moment. But she is really concerned about the many who are not represented by the pro-homosexual movement and about those who may have been tempted to believe its deceitful propaganda. She is also aware that the view that homosexual activity is equivalent to or as acceptable as the sexual expression of conjugal love has a direct impact on society's understanding of the nature and rights of the family and puts them in jeopardy.

10. It is deplorable that homosexual persons have been and are the object of violent malice in speech or in action. Such treatment deserves condemnation from the Church's pastors wherever it occurs. It reveals a kind of disregard for others which endangers the most fundamental principles of any healthy society. The intrinsic dignity of each person must always be respected in word, in action and in law.

But the proper reaction to crimes committed against homosexual persons should not be to claim that the homosexual condition is not disordered. When such a claim is made and when homosexual activity is consequently condoned or when legislation is introduced to protect behavior to which no one has any conceivable right, neither the Church nor society at large should be surprised when other distorted notions and practices gain ground, and irrational or violent reactions increase.

11. It has been argued that the homosexual orientation in certain cases is not the result of deliberate choice; and so the homosexual person would then have no choice but to behave in a homosexual fashion. Lacking freedom, such a person, even if engaged in homosexual activity, would not be culpable.

Here, the Church's wise moral tradition is necessary since it warns against generalizations in judging individual cases. In fact, circumstances may exist or may have existed in the past which would reduce or remove culpability of the individual in a given instance; or other circumstances may increase it. What is at all costs to be avoided is the unfounded and demeaning assumption that the sexual behavior of homosexual persons is always and totally compulsive and therefore inculpable. What is essential is that the fundamental liberty which characterizes the human person and gives him his dignity be recognized as belonging to the homosexual person as well. As in every conversion from evil, the abandonment of homosexual activity will require a profound collaboration of the individual with God's liberating grace.

12. What, then, are homosexual persons to do who seek to follow the Lord? Fundamentally, they are called to enact the will of God in their life by joining whatever sufferings and difficulties they experience in virtue of their condition to the sacrifice of the Lord's cross. That cross, for the believer, is a fruitful sacrifice since from that death come life and redemption. While any call to carry the cross or to understand a Christian's suffering in this way will predictably be met with bitter ridicule by some, it should be remembered that this is the way to eternal life for *all* who follow Christ.

It is, in effect, none other than the teaching of Paul the apostle to the Galatians when he says that the Spirit produces in the lives of the faithful "love, joy, peace, patience, kindness, goodness, trustfulness, gentleness, and self-control" (5.22) and further (Verse 24), "You cannot belong to Christ unless you crucify all your self-indulgent passions and desires."

It is easily misunderstood, however, if it is merely seen as pointless effort and self-denial. The cross *is* a denial of self, but in service to the will of God himself, who makes life come from death and empowers those who trust him to practice virtue in place of vice.

To celebrate the Pascal mystery it is necessary to let that mystery become imprinted in the fabric of daily life. To refuse to sacrifice one's own will in obedience to the will of the Lord is effectively to prevent salvation. Just as the cross was central to the expression of God's redemptive love for us in Jesus, so the conformity of the self-denial of homosexual men and women with the sacrifice of the Lord will constitute for them a source of self-giving which will save them from a way of life which constantly threatens to destroy them.

Christians who are homosexual are called, as all of us are, to a chaste life. As they dedicate their lives to understanding the nature of God's personal call to them, they will be able to celebrate the sacrament of penance more faithfully and receive the Lord's grace so freely offered there in order to convert their lives more fully to his way.

13. We recognize, of course, that in great measure the clear and successful communication of the Church's teaching to all the faithful and to society at large depends on the correct instruction and fidelity of her pastoral ministers. The bishops have the particularly grave responsibility to see to it that their assistants in the ministry, above all the priests, are rightly informed and personally disposed to bring the teaching of the Church in its integrity to everyone.

The characteristic concern and good will exhibited by many clergy and religious in their pastoral care for homosexual persons is admirable and, we hope, will not diminish. Such devoted ministers should have the confidence that they are faithfully following the will of the Lord by encouraging the homosexual person to lead a chaste life and by affirming that person's God-given dignity and worth.

14. With this in mind, this congregation wishes to ask bishops to be especially cautious of any programs which seek to pressure the Church to change her teaching, even while claiming not to do so. A careful examination of their public statements and the activities they promote reveals a studied ambiguity by which they attempt to mislead the pastors and the faithful. For example, they may present the teaching of the magisterium, but only as if it were an optional source for the formation of one's conscience. Its specific authority is not recognized. Some of these groups will use the word "Catholic" to describe either the organization or its intended members, yet they do not

defend and promote the teaching of the magisterium; indeed, they even openly attack it. While their members claim a desire to conform their lives to the teaching of Jesus, in fact they abandon the teaching of his Church. This contradictory action should not have the support of the bishops in any way.

15. We encourage the bishops, then, to provide pastoral care in full accord with the teaching of the Church for homosexual persons of their diocese. No authentic pastoral program will include organizations in which homosexual persons associate with each other without clearly stating that homosexual activity is immoral. A truly pastoral approach will appreciate the need for homosexual persons to avoid the near occasion of sin.

We would heartily encourage programs where these dangers are avoided. But we wish to make clear that departure from the Church's teaching or silence about it, in an effort to provide pastoral care, is neither caring nor pastoral. Only what is true can ultimately be pastoral. The neglect of the Church's position prevents homosexual men and women from receiving the care they need and deserve.

An authentic pastoral program will assist homosexual persons at all levels of the spiritual life: through the sacraments, and in particular through the frequent and sincere use of the sacrament of reconciliation, through prayer, witness, counsel, and individual care in such a way, the entire Christian community can come to recognize its own call to assist its brothers and sisters, without deluding them or isolating them.

16. From this multifaceted approach, there are numerous advantages to be gained, not the least of which is the realization that a homosexual person, as every human being, deeply needs to be nourished at many different levels simultaneously.

The human person, made in the image and likeness of God, can hardly be adequately described by a reductionist reference to his or her sexual orientation. Everyone living on the face of the earth has personal problems and difficulties, but challenges to growth, strengths, talents and gifts as well. Today the Church provides a badly needed context for the care of the human person as a "heterosexual" or a "homosexual" and insists that every person has a fundamental identity: the creature of God and, by grace, his child and heir to eternal life.

17. In bringing this entire matter to the bishop's attention, this congregation wishes to support their efforts to assure that the teaching of the Lord and his Church on this important question be communicated fully to the faithful.

In light of the points made above, they should decide for their own dioceses the extent to which an intervention on their part is indicated. In addition, should they consider it helpful, further coordinated action at the level of their national bishops' conference may be envisioned.

In a particular way we would ask the bishops to support, with the means at their disposal, the development of appropriate forms of pastoral care for homosexual persons. These would include the assistance of the psychological, sociological and medical sciences, in full accord with the teaching of the Church.

They are encouraged to call on the assistance of all Catholic theologians who, by teaching what the Church teaches and by deepening their reflections on the true meaning of human sexuality and Christian marriage with the virtues it engenders, will make an important contribution in this particular area of pastoral care.

The bishops are asked to exercise special care in the selection of pastoral ministers so that by their own high degree of spiritual and personal maturity and by their fidelity to the magisterium, they may be of real service to homosexual persons, promoting their health and well-being in the fullest sense. Such ministers will reject theological opinions which dissent from the teaching of the Church and which therefore cannot be used as guidelines for pastoral care.

We encourage the bishops to promote appropriate catechetical programs based on the truth about human sexuality in its relationships to the family as taught by the Church. Such programs should provide a good context within which to deal with the question of homosexuality.

This catechesis would also assist those families of homosexual persons to deal with this problem which affects them so deeply.

All support should be withdrawn from any organizations which seek to undermine the teachings of the Church, which are ambiguous about it or which neglect it entirely. Such support or even the semblance of such support can be gravely misinterpreted. Special attention should be given to the practice of scheduling services and to the use of Church buildings by these groups, including the facilities of Catholic schools and colleges. To some, such permission to use Church property may seem only just and charitable; but in reality it is contradictory to the purpose for which these institutions were founded, it is misleading and often scandalous.

In assessing proposed legislation, the bishops should keep as their upper-most concern the responsibility to defend and promote family life.

18. The Lord Jesus promised, "You shall know the truth and the truth shall set you free" (John 8.32). Scripture bids us to speak the truth in love (cf. Ephesians 4.15). The God who is at once truth and love calls the Church to minister to every man, woman, and child with pastoral solicitude of our compassionate Lord. It is in this spirit that we have addressed this letter to the bishops of the Church, with the hope that it will be of some help as they care for those whose suffering can only be intensified by error and lightened by truth.

During an audience granted to the undersigned prefect, His Holiness Pope John Paul II approved this letter, adopted in an ordinary session of the Congregation for the Doctrine of Faith, and ordered it to be published.

Given at Rome, Oct. 1, 1986.

Cardinal Joseph Ratzinger, prefect

Archbishop Alberto Bovone, secretary

Statement from the Pontifical Council for the Family, *The Truth and Meaning of Human Sexuality: Guidelines for Education Within the Family,* 1996, articles 104 and 125b

104. A particular problem that can appear during the process of sexual maturation is homosexuality, which is also spreading more and more in urbanized societies. This phenomenon must be presented with balanced judgment in the light of the documents of the church. Young people need to be helped to distinguish between the concepts of what is normal and abnormal, between subjective guilt and objective disorder, avoiding what would arouse hostility.

On the other hand, the structural and complementary orientation of sexuality must be well clarified in relation to marriage, procreation and Christian chastity. "Homosexual refers to relations between men and women who experience an exclusive or predominant sexual attraction toward persons of the same sex. It has taken a great variety of forms through the centuries and in different cultures. Its psychological genesis remains largely unexplained" (Catechism of the Catholic Church). A distinction must be made between a tendency that can be innate and acts of homosexuality that "are intrinsically disordered" and contrary to natural law (Pastoral Care of Homosexual Persons).

Especially when the practice of homosexual acts has not become a habit, many cases can benefit from appropriate therapy. In any case, persons in this situation must be accepted with respect, dignity, and delicacy, and all forms of unjust discrimination must be avoided. If parents notice the appearance of this tendency or of related behavior in their children during childhood or adolescence, they should seek help from expert qualified persons in order to obtain all possible assistance.

For most homosexual persons, this condition constitutes a trial. "They must be accepted with respect, compassion and sensitivity. Every sign of unjust discrimination in their regard should be avoided. These persons are called to fulfill God's will in their lives and, if they are Christians, to unite to the sacrifice of the Lord's cross the difficulties they may encounter from their condition." "Homosexual persons are called to chastity" (Catechism of the Catholic Church).

125. (b) Homosexuality should not be discussed before adolescence unless a specific serious problem has arisen in a particular situation. This subject must be presented only in terms of chastity, health, and "the truth about human sexuality in its relationship to the family as taught by the church" (Pastoral Care of Homosexual Persons).

Statement from the Vatican Congregation for the Doctrine of the Faith, *Declaration on Certain Questions Concerning Sexual Ethics ("Persona Humana"),* 1975, article 8

At the present time there are those who, basing themselves on the observations in the psychological order, have begun to judge indulgently, and even to excuse completely, homosexual relations between certain people. This they do in opposition to the constant teaching of the magisterium and to the moral sense of the Christian people.

A distinction is drawn, and it seems with some reason, between homosexuals whose tendency comes from a false education, from a lack of normal sexual development, from habit, from bad example, or from other similar causes, and is transitory or at least not incurable; and homosexuals who are definitively such because of some kind of innate instinct or a pathological constitution judged to be incurable.

In regard to this second category of subjects, some people conclude that their tendency is so natural that it justifies in their case homosexual relations within sincere communion of life and love analogous to marriage, insofar as such homosexuals feel capable of enduring a solitary life.

In the pastoral field, these homosexuals must certainly be treated with understanding and sustained in the hope of overcoming their personal difficulties and their inability to fit into society. Their culpability will be judged with prudence. But no pastoral method can be employed which would give moral justification to these acts on the grounds that they would be consonant with the condition of such people. For according to the objective moral order, homosexual relations are acts which lack an essential and indispensable finality. In sacred scripture they are condemned as a serious depravity and even presented as the sad consequence of rejecting God. This judgment of scripture does not of course permit us to conclude that all those who suffer from this anomaly are personally responsible for it, but it does attest to the fact that homosexual acts are intrinsically disordered and can in no case be approved of.

Statement from the United States Catholic Conference, *To Live in Christ Jesus: A Pastoral Reflection on the Moral Life*, 1976, no. 52

Some persons find themselves through no fault of their own to have a homosexual orientation. Homosexuals, like everyone else, should not suffer from prejudice against their basic human rights. They have a right to respect, friendship, and justice. They should have an active role in the Christian community. Homosexual activity, however, as distinguished from homosexual orientation, is morally wrong. Like heterosexual persons, homosexuals are called to give witness to chastity, avoiding, with God's grace, behavior which is wrong for them, just as nonmarital sexual relations are wrong for heterosexuals. Nonetheless, because heterosexuals can usually look forward to marriage, and homosexuals, while their orientation continues, might not, the Christian community should provide them a special degree of pastoral understanding and care.

Statement from the Vatican Congregation for Catholic Education, *Educational Guidance in Human Love: Outlines for Sex Education,* 1983, articles 101-103

101. Homosexuality, which impedes the person's acquisition of sexual maturity, whether from the individual point of view or the interpersonal, is a problem which must be faced in all objectivity by the pupil and the educator when the case presents itself.

"Pastorally, these homosexuals must be received with understanding and supported in the hope of overcoming their personal difficulties and their social maladaption. Their culpability will be judged with prudence; but no pastoral method can be employed which, holding that these acts conform to the conditions of these persons, accords them a moral justification.

"According to the objective moral order, homosexual relations are acts deprived of their essential and indispensable rule" (Vatican Congregation for the Doctrine of the Faith, 1975).

102. It will be the duty of the family and the teacher to seek first of all to identify the factors which drive toward homosexuality: to see if it is a question of physiological or psychological factors; if it be the result of false education or of a lack of normal sexual evolution; if it comes from a contracted habit or from bad example; or from other factors. More particularly, in seeking the causes of this disorder the family and the teacher will have to take account of the elements of judgment proposed by the ecclesiastical magisterium and be served by the contribution which various disciplines can offer. One must, in fact, investigate elements of diverse order: lack of affection, immatu-

rity, obsessive impulses, seduction, social isolation and other types of frustration, depravation in dress, license in shows and publications. In greater profundity lies the innate frailty of man and woman, the consequence of original sin; it can run to the loss of a sense of God and of man and woman, and have its repercussions in the sphere of sexuality.

103. The causes having been sought and understood, the family and the teacher will offer an efficacious help in the process of integral growth: welcoming with understanding, creating a climate of hope, encouraging the emancipation of the individual and his or her growth in self-control, promoting an authentic moral force toward conversion to the love of God and neighbor, suggesting—if necessary—medical-psychological assistance from persons attentive to and respectful of the teaching of the Church.

Statement from the Vatican Congregation for the Doctrine of the Faith, *The Catechism of the Catholic Church*, 1994, articles 2357-2359

2357 Homosexuality refers to relations between men or between women who experience an exclusive or predominant sexual attraction toward persons of the same sex. It has taken a great variety of forms through the centuries and in different cultures. Its psychological genesis remains largely unexplained. Basing itself on Sacred Scripture, which presents homosexual acts as acts of grave depravity (cf. Genesis 19.1-29; Romans 1.24-27; 1 Corinthians 6.10; 1 Timothy 1.10), tradition has always declared that "homosexual acts are intrinsically disordered" (Vatican Congregation for the Doctrine of the Faith, *Persona Humana*, 1975, article 8). They are contrary to the natural law. They close the sexual act to the gift of life. They do not proceed from a genuine affective and sexual complementarity. Under no circumstances can they be approved.

2358 The number of men and women who have deep-seated homosexual tendencies is not negligible. This inclination, which is objectively disordered, constitutes for most of them a trial. They must be accepted with respect, compassion, and sensitivity. Every sign of unjust discrimination in their regard should be avoided. These persons are called to fulfill God's will in their lives and, if they are Christians, to unite to the sacrifice of the Lord's Cross the difficulties they may encounter from their condition.

2359 Homosexual persons are called to chastity. By the virtues of self-mastery that teach them inner freedom, at times by the support of disinterested friendship, by prayer and sacramental grace, they can and should gradually and resolutely approach Christian perfection.

Appendix B

Tables from Survey Studies

Note that wording on item 3 changed from 1990 to 1995. For all tables, * indicates a statistically significant difference in responses (p < .05).

TABLE 1. Percentage of Kansas City–St. Joseph Confirmation Candidates Expressing Agreement with Statements As Compared by Sex in 1990

Statement	Total N=124	Males N=51	Females N=73
CATEGORY: NATURE AND MORALITY OF HOMOSEXUALITY			
1. Homosexuality is a disorder.	45.5%	68.6%	29.2%*
2. Sexual acts between persons of the same sex are morally wrong.	63.4%	88.2%	45.8%*
3. Being a gay or lesbian person is not morally wrong as long as the person does not engage in homosexual sex.	16.2%	11.8%	21.1%*
4. Gay and lesbian people are not responsible for their sexual preferences.	24.0%	15.7%	29.4%*
CATEGORY: RIGHTS OF GAY AND LESBIAN PEOPLE			
5. All people (gay, lesbian, and heterosexual) are children of God.	87.0%	78.4%	93.2%*
6. Gay and lesbian people have basic human rights.	81.3%	70.6%	88.9%*
7. Gay and lesbian people deserve respect.	67.5%	41.2%	86.1%*
8. Gay and lesbian people deserve friendship.	74.0%	52.9%	88.9%*
9. Gay and lesbian people deserve justice.	74.0%	52.9%	88.9%*
10. Words such as "fag" and "dyke" as well as jokes about gay and lesbian people are not acceptable.	43.4%	21.6%	52.5%*

Statement	Total N=124	Males N=51	Females N=73
11. Physical violence against gay and lesbian people is not acceptable.	82.1%	62.8%	95.8%*

CATEGORY: CHURCH RESPONSIBILITIES TO GAY
AND LESBIAN PEOPLE

	Total	Males	Females
12. Church leaders should speak out against derogatory terms, jokes, and violence directed against gay and lesbian people when they occur.	51.2%	39.2%	59.7%*
13. The Church should treat gay and lesbian people with understanding.	62.6%	41.2%	77.8%*
14. The Church should have special programs for gay and lesbian people.	22.1%	17.6%	25.4%*
15. The Church should help gay and lesbian people move more into society.	30.9%	15.7%	41.7%*
16. Gay and lesbian people should have an active role in the Christian community.	40.7%	25.5%	51.4%*

TABLE 2. Pearson Correlation Between Agreement with Catholic Church Teaching and Years in Catholic Education (Parish Programs or Catholic Schools) in Kansas City–St. Joseph Confirmation Candidates in 1990

Category	Total	Males	Females
Nature and morality of homosexuality	+.13	+.68 *	+.00
Rights of gay and lesbian people	-.07	-.24	+.10
Church responsibilities to gay and lesbian people	+.16	+.28 *	-.11

TABLE 3. Percentage of Catholic University Incoming Freshmen Expressing Agreement with Statements As Compared by Sex in 1995

Statement	Total N=103	Males N=32	Females N=71

CATEGORY: NATURE AND MORALITY OF HOMOSEXUALITY

	Total	Males	Females
1. Homosexuality is a disorder.	16.5%	34.4%	8.7%*
2. Sexual acts between persons of the same sex are morally wrong.	40.7%	68.8%	28.2%*
3. Being sexually attracted to persons of the same sex is not morally wrong.	67.0%	46.9%	76.1%*
4. Gay and lesbian people are not responsible for their sexual preferences.	43.7%	25.0%	52.1%*

CATEGORY: RIGHTS OF GAY AND LESBIAN PEOPLE

5. All people (gay, lesbian, and heterosexual) are children of God.	87.0%	75.5%	91.3%*
6. Gay and lesbian people have basic human rights.	94.2%	81.3%	100.0% *
7. Gay and lesbian people deserve respect.	79.4%	74.2%	81.7%*
8. Gay and lesbian people deserve friendship.	95.0%	78.2%	100.0%*
9. Gay and lesbian people deserve justice.	92.1%	77.4%	100.0%*
10. Words such as "fag" and "dyke" as well as jokes about gay and lesbian people are not acceptable.	78.6%	46.9%	92.9%*
11. Physical violence against gay and lesbian people is not acceptable.	95.1%	84.4%	100.0%*

CATEGORY: CHURCH RESPONSIBILITIES TO GAY AND LESBIAN PEOPLE

12. Church leaders should speak out against derogatory terms, jokes, and violence directed against gay and lesbian people when they occur.	70.6%	51.7%	78.9%*
13. The Church should treat gay and lesbian people with understanding.	75.2%	43.4%	88.8%*
14. The Church should have special programs for gay and lesbian people.	32.7%	18.8%	39.1%*
15. The Church should help gay and lesbian people move more into society.	42.6%	31.3%	47.8%*
16. Gay and lesbian people should have an active role in the Christian community.	63.4%	35.5%	75.7%*

TABLE 4. Percentage of Catholic University Incoming Freshmen Expressing Agreement with Statements as Compared Between Graduates from Catholic High Schools and Graduates from Non-Catholic High Schools in 1995

Statement	Catholic School N=44	Non-Catholic N=59

CATEGORY: NATURE AND MORALITY OF HOMOSEXUALITY

Statement	Catholic School N=44	Non-Catholic N=59
1. Homosexuality is a disorder.	14.3%	23.8%*
2. Sexual acts between persons of the same sex are morally wrong.	34.1%	45.7%*
3. Being sexually attracted to persons of the same sex is not morally wrong.	79.5%	57.6%*
4. Gay and lesbian people are not responsible for their sexual preferences.	45.5%	42.4%

CATEGORY: RIGHTS OF GAY AND LESBIAN PEOPLE

Statement	Catholic School N=44	Non-Catholic N=59
5. All people (gay, lesbian, and heterosexual) are children of God.	88.6%	85.7%

Statement	Catholic School N=44	Non-Catholic N=59
6. Gay and lesbian people have basic human rights.	97.7%	91.6%*
7. Gay and lesbian people deserve respect.	90.9%	87.9%
8. Gay and lesbian people deserve friendship.	95.4%	91.5%
9. Gay and lesbian people deserve justice.	93.2%	92.8%
10. Words such as "fag" and "dyke" as well as jokes about gay and lesbian people are not acceptable.	77.2%	72.4%
11. Physical violence against gay and lesbian people is not acceptable.	97.7%	93.2%

CATEGORY: CHURCH RESPONSIBILITIES TO GAY
AND LESBIAN PEOPLE

12. Church leaders should speak out against derogatory terms, jokes, and violence directed against gay and lesbian people when they occur.	76.7%	66.1%*
13. The Church should treat gay and lesbian people with understanding.	86.1%	67.3%*
14. The Church should have special programs for gay and lesbian people.	45.4%	22.8%*
15. The Church should help gay and lesbian people move more into society.	52.2%	35.1%*
16. Gay and lesbian people should have an an active role in the Christian community.	61.4%	56.1%

TABLE 5. Percentage of Catholic University Incoming Freshmen Expressing Agreement with Statements As Compared Between Graduates from Coeducational Catholic High Schools and Graduates from Unisex Catholic High Schools in 1995

Statement	Catholic Coed N=21	Catholic Unisex N=23

CATEGORY: NATURE AND MORALITY OF HOMOSEXUALITY

1. Homosexuality is a disorder.	10.6%	17.3%*
2. Sexual acts between persons of the same sex are morally wrong.	38.1%	30.4%
3. Being sexually attracted to persons of the same sex is not morally wrong.	85.7%	73.9%*
4. Gay and lesbian people are not responsible for their sexual preferences.	47.6%	39.1%

CATEGORY: RIGHTS OF GAY AND LESBIAN PEOPLE

5. All people (gay, lesbian, and heterosexual) are children of God.	95.2%	82.6%*

6. Gay and lesbian people have basic human 100.0%   95.7%*
   rights.
7. Gay and lesbian people deserve respect.   95.2%   86.9%*
8. Gay and lesbian people deserve friendship. 100.0%   91.4%*
9. Gay and lesbian people deserve justice.   100.0%   87.0%*
10. Words such as "fag" and "dyke" as well as   85.7%   69.5%*
    jokes about gay and lesbian people are not
    acceptable.
11. Physical violence against gay and lesbian 100.0%   95.7%*
    people is not acceptable.

CATEGORY: CHURCH RESPONSIBILITIES TO GAY
AND LESBIAN PEOPLE

12. Church leaders should speak out against   90.5%   68.2%*
    derogatory terms, jokes, and violence
    directed against gay and lesbian people
    when they occur.
13. The Church should treat gay and lesbian   90.5%   81.8%*
    people with understanding.
14. The Church should have special programs   57.1%   34.7%*
    for gay and lesbian people.
15. The Church should help gay and lesbian   61.9%   43.4%*
    people move more into society.
16. Gay and lesbian people should have   71.4%   73.9%
    an active role in the Christian community.

References

Aguero, J. E., Bloch, L., and Byrne, D. (1985). The relationship among sexual beliefs, attitudes, experience, and homophobia. In De Cecco, J. P. (ed.) *Bashers, baiters, and bigots: Homophobia in American society* (pp. 95-108). Binghamton, NY: Harrington Park Press.

Aitken, J. E. (1993). "Privileges: A student activity designed to increase interpersonal communication competence regarding gay and lesbian concerns." Paper presented at the Annual Meeting of the Speech Communication Association, Miami, FL, November.

Barbetta, K. C. (1989). Heterosexual bias and stereotyping of homosexual couples: A demonstration through information processing and video evaluation. *Dissertation Abstracts International 48*(10), 3150B.

Bennett, E. L. (1992). The psychology and developmental process of maintaining a positive lesbian identity. *Dissertation Abstracts International 52*(11), 3150B.

Black, K. N. and Stevenson, M. R. (1985). The relationship of self-report sex-role characteristics and attitudes toward homosexuality. In De Cecco, J. P. (ed.) *Bashers, baiters, and bigots: Homophobia in American society* (pp. 83-94). Binghamton, NY: Harrington Park Press.

Bleich, D. (1989). Homophobia and sexism as popular values. *Feminist Teacher 4*(2-3), 21-28.

Bohn, T. R. (1985). Homophobic violence: Implications for social work practice. In Schoenberg, R., Goldberg, R. S., and Shore, D. A. (eds.) *With compassion toward some: Homosexuality and social work in America* (pp. 91-114). Binghamton, NY: Harrington Park Press.

Bullough, V. and Bullough, B. (1978). "Nineteenth century English homosexual teachers: The up front and back stage performance." Paper presented at the Annual Meeting of the American Sociological Association, San Francisco, CA, September.

Cass, V. C. (1979). Homosexual identity formation: A theoretical model. *Journal of Homosexuality 4*(3), 219-235.

Cass, V. C. (1984). Homosexual identity formation: Testing a theoretical model. *Journal of Sex Research 20*(2), 143-167.

The Child Welfare League of America (1991). *Serving gay and lesbian youths: The role of child welfare agencies.* Washington, DC: The Child Welfare League of America.

D'Augelli, A. R. (1989). Homophobia in a university community: Views of prospective resident assistants. *Journal of College Student Development 30*(6), 546-552.

D'Augelli, A. R. and Rose, M. L. (1990). Homophobia in a university community: Attitudes and experiences of university freshmen. *Journal of College Student Development 31*(6), 484-491.

de Monteflores, C. and Schultz, S. J. (1978). Coming out: Similarities and differences for lesbians and gay men. *Journal of Social Issues, 34,* 59-72.

DeCrescenzo, T. A. (1985). Homophobia: A study of the attitudes of mental health practitioners toward homosexuality. In Schoenberg, R., Goldberg, R. S., and Shore, D. A. (eds.) *With compassion toward some: Homosexuality and social work in America* (pp. 115-136). Binghamton, NY: Harrington Park Press.

Densley, S. R. (1991). The evolution of the philosophy of Catholic schools: An analysis of recent church documents, 1929-1990. *Dissertation Abstracts International, 51*(11), 3664A.

DeVine, J. L. (1985). A systematic inspection of affectional preference orientation and the family of origin. In Schoenberg, R., Goldberg, R. S., and Shore, D. A. (eds.) *With compassion toward some: Homosexuality and social work in America* (pp. 9-18). Binghamton, NY: Harrington Park Press.

DiGiacomo, J. (1993). *Morality and youth: Fostering Christian identity.* Kansas City, MO: Sheed and Ward.

Durby, D. D. (1994). Gay, lesbian, and bisexual youth. In DeCrescenzo, T. (ed.) *Helping gay and lesbian youth: New policies, new programs, new practice* (pp. 1-38). Binghamton, NY: Harrington Park Press.

DuVal, M. W. (1991). The effects of a value-centered curriculum on the attitudes of Catholic high school seniors toward the role of women, economic poverty, and racial injustice. *Dissertation Abstracts International, 52*(5), 1623A.

Ellis, D. D. (1989). The impact of the AIDS epidemic stigma on homophobia and sex-role rigidity of time. *Dissertation Abstracts International 50*(7), 1943A.

Fee, J. L., Greeley, A. M., McCready, W. C., and Sullivan, T. A. (1981). *Young Catholics in the United States and Canada: A report to the Knights of Columbus.* New York: William H. Sadlier, Inc.

Finn, P. and McNeil, T. (1987). The response of the criminal justice system to bias crime. Washington, DC: U.S. Department of Justice.

Forliti, J. (1984). *Growing together: An opportunity for young adolescents and their parents.* Washington, DC: National Catholic Education Association.

Friend, R. A. (1993). Choices, not closets: Heterosexism and homophobia in schools. In Weis, L. and Fine, M. (eds.) *Beyond silenced voices: Class, race, and gender in United States schools* (pp. 209-236). Albany, NY: State University of New York Press.

Gevelinger, M. E. and Zimmerman, L. (1997). How Catholic schools are creating a safe climate for gay and lesbian students. *Educational Leadership 55*(2) October, 66-68.

Gibson, P. (1989). Gay male and lesbian youth suicide. In Feinleib, M. (ed.) *Report of the secretary's task force on youth suicide,* Vol. 3 (pp. 3110-3142). Washington, DC: U.S. Department of Health and Human Services.

Gover, J. (1994). Gay youth in the family. *Journal of Emotional and Behavioral Problems 2*(4), 34-38.

Greeley, G. (1994). Service organizations for gay and lesbian youth. In DeCrescenzo, T. (ed.) *Helping gay and lesbian youth: New policies, new programs, new practice* (pp. 111-130). Binghamton, NY: Harrington Park Press.

Grieger, I. and Ponterotto, J. G. (1988). Students' knowledge of AIDS and their attitudes toward gay men and lesbian women. *Journal of College Student Development 29*(5), 415-422.

Hansen, G. L. (1982). Measuring prejudice against homosexuality (homosexism) among college students: A new scale. *Journal of Social Psychology 117(2),* 233-236.

Herdt, G. and Boxer, A. (1993). *Children of Horizons: How gay and lesbian teens are leading a new way out of the closet.* Boston: Beacon Press.

Herek, G. M. (1985a). Attitudes toward lesbians and gay men: A factor-analytic study. In De Cecco, J. P. (ed.) *Bashers, baiters, and bigots: Homophobia in American society* (pp. 39-52). Binghamton, NY: Harrington Park Press.

Herek, G. M. (1985b). Beyond "homophobia": A social psychological perspective on attitudes toward lesbians and gay men. In De Cecco, J. P. (ed.) *Bashers, baiters, and bigots: Homophobia in American society* (pp. 1-22). Binghamton, NY: Harrington Park Press.

Hetrick, E. S. and Martin, A. D. (1987). Developmental issues and their resolution for gay and lesbian adolescents. *Journal of Homosexuality, 14*(1/2), 25-43.

Hunt, B. B. (1993). Counselor education students: Their knowledge, attitudes, and beliefs regarding gay, lesbian, and bisexual clients. *Dissertation Abstracts International 54*(5), 1679A.

Hunter, J. (1990). Violence against lesbian and gay male youths. *Journal of Interpersonal Violence 5*(3), September, 295-300.

Innes, D. L. (1992). Mechanisms by which values are imparted in a Catholic elementary school: A qualitative study. *Dissertation Abstracts International 53*(3), 667A.

Jackson, D. and Sullivan, R. (1994). Developmental implications of homophobia for lesbian and gay adolescents: Issues in policy and practice. In DeCrescenzo, T. (ed.) *Helping gay and lesbian youth: New policies, new programs, new practice* (pp. 93-110). Binghamton, NY: Harrington Park Press.

Jennes, V. (1992). Coming out: Lesbian identities and the categorization problem. In Plummer, K. (ed.) *Modern homosexualities: Fragments of lesbian and gay experience* (pp. 65-74). New York: Routledge.

Johnson, T. W. (1992). Predicting parental response to a son or daughter's homosexuality. *Dissertation Abstracts International 53*(6), 1847A.

Kielwasser, A. P. and Wolf, M. A. (1991). "The sound (and sight) of silence: Notes on television and the communication ecology of adolescent homosexuality." Paper presented at the Annual Meeting of the Western States Communication Association, Phoenix, AZ, February.

Kielwasser, A. P. and Wolf, M. A. (1992). Mainstream television, adolescent homosexuality, and significant silence. *Critical Studies in Mass Communication* 9(4), 350-373.

Kissen, R. M. (1991). "Listening to gay and lesbian teenagers." Paper presented at the Annual Meeting of the National Council of teachers of English, Seattle, WA, November.

Kissen, R. M. (1993). "Voices from the classroom closet: Lesbian and gay teachers talk about their lives." Paper presented at the Annual Meeting of the American Educational Research Association, Atlanta, GA, April.

Kite, M. E. (1985). Sex differences in attitudes toward homosexuals: A meta-analytic review. In De Cecco, J. P. (ed.) *Bashers, baiters, and bigots: Homophobia in American society* (pp. 69-82). Binghamton, NY: Harrington Park Press.

Kline, M. T. (1991). Human sexuality programs in Catholic secondary schools in the 80s. *Dissertation Abstracts International, 51*(11), 3689A.

Lipkin, A. S. (1992). Project 10: Gay and lesbian students find acceptance in their school community. *Teaching Tolerance 1*(2), 24-27.

Mallon, G. P. (1994). Counseling strategies with gay and lesbian youth. In DeCrescenzo, T. (ed.) *Helping gay and lesbian youth: New policies, new programs, new practice* (pp. 75-92). Binghamton, NY: Harrington Park Press.

Massachusetts Governor's Commission on Gay and Lesbian Youth (1993). *Making schools safe for gay and lesbian youth: Breaking silence in schools and families.* Massachusetts Governor's Commission on Gay and Lesbian Youth: Boston.

McAuley, E. N. and Mattieson, M. (1986). *Faith without form: Beliefs of Catholic youth.* Kansas City, MO: Sheed and Ward.

McClerren, B. L. (1992). An exploratory study concerning homophobia among the clergy and its relationship to attitudes toward acquired immune deficiency syndrome. *Dissertation Abstracts International 52*(4), 3833A.

McCleskey, K. E. (1991). The effects of a special training program about homosexuality on the knowledge and attitudes of counselor trainees. *Dissertation Abstracts International 52*(4), 1213A.

McClintock, M. (1992). Sharing lesbian, gay, and bisexual life experiences. *Journal of Experiential Education 15*(3), 51-55.

McDevitt, T. M. (1987). "Attitudes toward individuals with AIDS and homosexuals." Paper presented at the Annual Convention of the American Psychological Association, New York, NY, August.

McNamara, P. H. (1992). *Conscience first, tradition second: A study of young American Catholics.* Albany, NY: State University of New York Press.

Millham, J., San Miguel, C. L., and Kellog, R. (1976). A factor-analytical conceptualization of attitudes toward male and female homosexuals. *Journal of Homosexuality 2*(1), 3-10.

The National Gay Task Force (1984). *Anti-gay/lesbian victimization.* New York: The National Gay Task Force.

Newman, B. S. (1985). Development of heterosexuals' attitudes toward lesbians. *Dissertation Abstracts International 47*(5), 1881A.

Nugent, R. (1989). Homosexuality and seminary candidates. In Gramick, J. (ed.) *Homosexuality in the priesthood and religious life* (pp. 200-218). New York: Crossroad Publishing.

O'Neil, J. M. (1982). "Fear of femininity scale (FOFS): Men's gender role conflict." Paper presented at the Annual Convention of the American Psychological Association, Washington, DC, August.

O'Neil, J. M. (1984). "Data on college men's gender role conflict and strain." Paper presented at the Annual Convention of the American Psychological Association, Toronto, Canada, August.

Plasek, J. W. and Allard, J. (1985). Misconceptions of homophobia. In De Cecco, J. P. (ed.) *Bashers, baiters, and bigots: Homophobia in American society* (pp. 23-38). Binghamton, NY: Harrington Park Press.

Plummer, K. (1975). *Sexual stigma: An interactionist account.* London: Routledge and Kegan Paul.

Ponse, B. (1978). *Identities in the lesbian world: The social construction of self.* Westport, CT: Greenwood Press.

Ponse, B. (1984). The problematic meanings of lesbians. In Douglas, J. D. (ed.) *The sociology of deviance* (pp. 24-33). Newton, MA: Allyn & Bacon.

Pontifical Council for the Family (1996). *The truth and meaning of human sexuality: Guidelines for education within the family.* Rome.

Pope John Paul II (1979). *On catechesis in our time.* Rome.

Pope John Paul II (1981). *On the Family.* Rome.

Pope Pius XI (1929). *Christian education of youth.* Rome.

Pope Pius XI (1935). *On better care for catechetical teaching.* Rome.

Pope Pius XII (1951). *Council to teaching sisters.* Rome.

Reed, D. B. (1992). "Gay youth in public high schools: Invisible diversity." Paper presented at the Annual Meeting of the University Council for Educational Administration, Minneapolis, MN, October/November.

Reed, D. B. (1993). "High school gay youth: Invisible diversity." Paper presented at the Annual Meeting of the American Education Research Association, Atlanta, GA, April.

Reed, D. B. (1994). "The sexualized context of American public high schools." Paper presented at the Annual Meeting of the American Education Research Association, New Orleans, LA, April.

Reinhardt, B. M. (1995). Effects of gay and lesbian speaker panels on self-report measures of individual homophobia. *Dissertation Abstracts International 55*(10), 314A.

Remafedi, G. (1993). The impact of training on school professionals' knowledge, beliefs, and behavior regarding HIV/AIDS and adolescent homosexuality. *Journal of School Health 63*(3), 153-157.

Remafedi, G., Farrow, J., and Deisher, R. (1991). Risk factors for attempted suicide in gay and bisexual youth. *Pediatrics 87*(6), June, 869-875.

Rudolph, J. R. (1988). The effects of a multimodel seminar on mental health practitioners' attitudes toward homosexuality, authoritarianism, and counseling effectiveness. *Dissertation Abstracts International 49*(7), 2873B.

Rullman, L. J. (1991). A legal history: University recognition of homosexual organizations. *Association of College Unions International: Bulletin 59*(2), 4-9.

Russell, D. C. and Ellis, J. B. (1993). "Religiosity, gender, sex anxiety, and AIDS attitudes as they affect attitudes toward homosexuals." Paper presented at the Annual Meeting of the Southeastern Psychological Association, Atlanta, GA, March.

Rybicki, W. N. (1995). The gay identity in the age of AIDS. *Dissertation Abstracts International 56*(3), 1134A.

Saint Pius X (1905). *Handing on Christian doctrine by teaching.* Rome.

Salmi, R. P. (1994). Changing attitudes toward lesbian women and gay men among college freshmen: The effects of a campus intervention program. *Dissertation Abstracts International 55*(6), 1425A.

Savin-Williams, R. C. (1989). Parental influence on the self-esteem of gay and lesbian youths: A reflected appraisal method. In Herdt, G. (ed.) *Gay and lesbian youth* (pp. 93-110). Binghamton, NY: Harrington Park Press.

Savin-Williams, R. C. (1990). *Gay and lesbian youth: Expressions of identity.* New York: Hemisphere Publishing Corporation.

Schneider, M. (1989). Sappho was a right-on adolescent: Growing up lesbian. In Herdt, G. (ed.) *Gay and lesbian youth* (pp. 111-130). Binghamton, NY: Harrington Park Press.

Sears, J. T. (1988). "Attitudes, experiences, and feelings of guidance counselors in working with homosexual students: A report on the quality of school life for southern gay and lesbian students." Paper presented at the Annual Meeting of the Educational Research Association, New Orleans, LA, April.

Second Vatican Council (1965). *Declaration on Christian education.* Rome.

Serdahely, W. J. and Ziemba, G. J. (1985). Changing homophobic attitudes through college sexuality education. In De Cecco, J. P. (ed.) *Bashers, baiters, and bigots: Homophobia in American society* (pp. 109-116). Binghamton, NY: Harrington Park Press.

Troiden, R. R. (1988). *Gay and lesbian identity: A sociological analysis* (pp. 43-74). Dix Hills, NY: General Hall.

Troiden, R. R. (1989). The formation of homosexual identities. In Herdt, G. (ed.) *Gay and lesbian youth.* Binghamton, NY: Harrington Park Press.

United States Catholic Conference (1968). *Human life in our day: A collective pastoral letter of the American hierarchy.* Washington, DC.

United States Catholic Conference (1972). *To teach as Jesus did: A pastoral message on Catholic education.* Washington, DC.

United States Catholic Conference (1973a). *Basic teachings for Catholic religious education.* Washington, DC.

United States Catholic Conference (1973b). *Principles to guide confessors in questions of homosexuality.* Washington, DC.

United States Catholic Conference (1976a). *Teach them.* Washington, DC.

United States Catholic Conference (1976b). *To live in Christ Jesus: A pastoral reflection on the moral life.* Washington, DC.

United States Catholic Conference (1979). *Sharing the light of faith: National catechetical directory for Catholics of the United States.* Washington, DC.

United States Catholic Conference (1980). *Catholic higher education and the church's pastoral mission.* Washington, DC.

United States Catholic Conference (1981). *Education in human sexuality for Christians: Guidelines for discussion and planning.* Washington, DC.

United States Catholic Conference (1990). *Guidelines for doctrinally sound catechetical materials.* Washington, DC.

United States Catholic Conference (1991). *Human sexuality: A Catholic perspective for education and lifelong learning.* Washington, DC.

United States Catholic Conference, NCCB Committee on Marriage and Family (1997). *Always our children: Pastoral message to parents of homosexual children and suggestions for pastoral ministers.* Washington, DC.

Vatican Congregation for Catholic Education (1977). *The Catholic school.* Rome.

Vatican Congregation for Catholic Education (1983). *Educational guidance in human love: Outlines for sex education.* Rome.

Vatican Congregation for Catholic Education (1988). *The religious dimension of education in a Catholic school: Guidelines for reflection and renewal.* Rome.

Vatican Congregation for the Clergy (1971). *General catechetical directory.* Rome.

Vatican Congregation for the Doctrine of the Faith (1975). *Declaration on certain questions concerning sexual ethics (Persona Humana).* Rome.

Vatican Congregation for the Doctrine of the Faith (1986). *Letter to the bishops of the Catholic Church on the pastoral care of homosexual persons.* Rome.

Vatican Congregation for the Doctrine of the Faith (1992). *Some considerations concerning the response to legislative proposals on the non-discrimination of homosexual persons.* Rome.

Vatican Congregation for the Doctrine of the Faith (1994). *Catechism of the Catholic Church.* Rome.

Vergara, T. L. (1985). Meeting the needs of sexual minority youth: One program's response. In Schoenberg, R., Goldberg, R. S., and Shore, D. A. (eds.) *With compassion toward some: Homosexuality and social work in America* (pp. 19-38). Binghamton, NY: Harrington Park Press.

Walters, A. S. (1990). "The influence of homophobia and knowledge of AIDS on empathy for persons with AIDS." Paper presented at the Annual Meeting of the American Association of Sex Education, Counselors, and Therapists, Arlington, VA, February.

Watter, D. H. (1985). The relationship between teaching methodology, gender, and religiosity on the positive modification of attitudes toward homosexuality among heterosexuals in a college population. *Dissertation Abstracts International 47*(1), 94A.

Weinberg, G. (1972). *Society and the healthy homosexual.* New York: St. Martin's Press.

Wells, J. W. (1989). Teaching about gay and lesbian sexual and affectional orientation using explicit films to reduce homophobia. *Journal of Humanistic Education and Development 28*(1), 18-34.

Witlock, K. and Kamel, R. (1989). *Bridges of respect: Creating support for lesbian and gay youth.* Philadelphia: The American Friends Service Committee.

Wool, P. C. (1987). The development of a Bible study curriculum for the local church related to the issue of homosexuality. *Dissertation Abstracts International 48*(5), 1230A.

Index

Page numbers followed by the letter "t" indicate tables.

Order Your Own Copy of
This Important Book for Your Personal Library!

BEING GAY AND LESBIAN IN A CATHOLIC HIGH SCHOOL
Beyond the Uniform

_____in hardbound at $29.95 (ISBN: 1-56023-182-3)
_____in softbound at $17.95 (ISBN: 1-56023-183-1)

COST OF BOOKS_____

OUTSIDE USA/CANADA/
MEXICO: ADD 20%____

POSTAGE & HANDLING_____
*(US: $4.00 for first book & $1.50
for each additional book)*
*Outside US: $5.00 for first book
& $2.00 for each additional book)*

SUBTOTAL_____

in Canada: add 7% GST____

STATE TAX____
*(NY, OH & MIN residents, please
add appropriate local sales tax)*

FINAL TOTAL____
*(If paying in Canadian funds,
convert using the current
exchange rate, UNESCO
coupons welcome.)*

❏ **BILL ME LATER:** ($5 service charge will be added)
(Bill-me option is good on US/Canada/Mexico orders only;
not good to jobbers, wholesalers, or subscription agencies.)

❏ Check here if billing address is different from
shipping address and attach purchase order and
billing address information.

Signature_____

❏ **PAYMENT ENCLOSED: $**_____

❏ **PLEASE CHARGE TO MY CREDIT CARD.**

❏ Visa ❏ MasterCard ❏ AmEx ❏ Discover
❏ Diner's Club ❏ Eurocard ❏ JCB

Account # _____

Exp. Date_____

Signature_____

Prices in US dollars and subject to change without notice.

NAME_____
INSTITUTION_____
ADDRESS_____
CITY_____
STATE/ZIP_____
COUNTRY_____ COUNTY (NY residents only)_____
TEL_____ FAX_____
E-MAIL_____

May we use your e-mail address for confirmations and other types of information? ❏ Yes ❏ No
We appreciate receiving your e-mail address and fax number. Haworth would like to e-mail or fax special
discount offers to you, as a preferred customer. **We will never share, rent, or exchange your e-mail address
or fax number.** We regard such actions as an invasion of your privacy.

Order From Your Local Bookstore or Directly From
The Haworth Press, Inc.
10 Alice Street, Binghamton, New York 13904-1580 • USA .
TELEPHONE: 1-800-HAWORTH (1-800-429-6784) / Outside US/Canada: (607) 722-5857
FAX: 1-800-895-0582 / Outside US/Canada: (607) 722-6362
E-mail: getinfo@haworthpressinc.com
PLEASE PHOTOCOPY THIS FORM FOR YOUR PERSONAL USE.
www.HaworthPress.com

BOF00